'What the world teaches c… odds with God's commands… Chris Richards and Dr Liz … resource: one that encourage… and thus equipped to discern … true. By clearly defining and explaining six key issues at the forefront of our culture, and by guiding teens through Scripture passages that address each of these topics, Richards and Jones help to prepare teens to live in such a way that is honouring to God.'

Erika Allen, author of ESV Prayer Journals

'Liz and Chris bring not only a clarity of teaching, but also a vulnerability of spirit as they share with the reader key biblical principles, on some of the most contested issues of our generation. As a young person reading this, wrestle with these chapters, even if their content may seem counter cultural, and unearth some wonderful truths as you pray about following Christ in your relationships and actions.'

Steve Beegoo, Head of Education at Christian Concern

'I cannot speak highly enough of this timely book. It is unafraid to tackle the issues of our day, which are of grave concern to most right-thinking people. Fact-based, Biblio-centric, warm-hearted, clear thinking, it is a must read for all teens and pre-teens and, or preferably with, their parents.'

Ann Benton, author of *Parenting Against the Tide* and *The Fruitful Home*

'In a world that values individual preference and feelings above all else, this book reminds us that God's ways are right and good. A wide range of subjects are covered in a clear, faithful and sensitive way. There is enough detail to warn where needed, without creating unhelpful curiosity. Our young people are looking for straightforward answers on these topics. Dr Chris Richards and Dr Liz Jones are trusted sources for biblical principles and godly wisdom.'

Matthew Seymour, Pastor, Emmanuel Church, Leamington Spa

Challenges
to Living
God's way

what about abortion?

is homosexuality okay?

Challenges to Living God's way

is co-habitation bad?

how do I avoid porn?

what if I have transgender friends?

is feminism good?

Dr Chris Richards + Dr Liz Jones

10 Publishing
a division of 10 of those.com

First published in Great Britain in 2022

British Cataloguing in Publication Data
A record for this book is available from the British Library

ISBN: 978-1-783973-38-5

Designed by Jude May
Cover image © Aleksei Lagunov | iStock

Printed in Denmark

Evangelical Press (EP Books), an imprint of 10Publishing
Unit C, Tomlinson Road, Leyland, PR25 2DY, England
epbooks@10ofthose.com
www.epbooks.org

1 3 5 7 10 8 6 4 2

Contents

1

Laying good foundations

The aim of this book is to help you navigate some difficult issues which have become part of our society in the last 70 years. During this time we have become a more 'secular' society. 'Secular' describes a society where God has been rejected, with the result that many of God's laws, which used to be the foundation of Western society, have been put aside one by one. People are now increasingly allowed to do whatever they want to do, which is not necessarily good. This was the chaotic situation at the end of the Old Testament book of Judges, where it says, 'Everyone did what was right in his own eyes' (Judges 21:25).

This way of thinking has especially affected our society's attitude towards marriage and sexual relationships. It is reflected in our laws, in mainstream media and on social media, which now reject the Bible's teaching that marriage is a lifelong relationship between a man and a woman. Many people in our society encourage sexual intimacy outside marriage, rather than seeing it as a special gift from God, only to be shared within marriage.

As young people, sooner or later, you will face challenges in this area. You will need to be *wise* not to be taken in because sometimes these challenges come in very subtle ways (for example, assumptions made in what you are taught at school), and you will need to be *strong* because sometimes the challenges come in very pressurising ways (through your friends and peers, for example). We have written this book to help prepare you for this.

The first few chapters focus on six big moral issues. Each of these chapters concludes with a testimony showing how God has helped someone facing the issue. The last three chapters of the book discuss what the Bible says about sexual purity and marriage. This will help you to honour God in your personal life.

The writer of the Bible book of Ecclesiastes talks about how he did not find satisfaction and pleasure in all the things that this world offered him, even though he was very wealthy and powerful. In the final chapter, he makes a particular call to young people with these words:

> *Remember also your Creator in the days of your youth… Fear God and keep his commandments, for this is the whole duty of man.* (Ecclesiastes 12:1, 13)

Dr Chris Richards + Dr Liz Jones

As two paediatricians, we have seen many young people damaged, and many families destroyed, by wrong decisions made in sexual relationships. You have much of your life ahead of you – so remember God, your Creator, and keep his commandments at the centre of your life. This will encourage you to invest in the future rather than in what appears to give pleasure in the short term. Although it won't always seem like it, God's ways really are good. He made us, he loves us and he does know what's best for us. We hope that this book will help you think through these issues, and realise that this is true.

Six big issues

2

Cohabitation

Cohabitation is also called 'living together'. It describes a couple sharing a home and being sexually intimate with each other when they are not married. It is seen by many as a stage before marriage or as an alternative to marriage. Cohabitation has become very common in our society. It has almost become accepted as a necessary stage in a relationship that is moving towards long-term commitment.

Fact box

- *In the UK, cohabiting couple families were the fastest-growing family type over the last decade with an increase of nearly 20% from 2.86 million in 2011 to 3.43 million in 2021.*[1] *In the US, the numbers are also growing, with an increase from 7.6 million to 9.6 million over the same period.*[2]

- *Over 80% of marriages in England and Wales take place when the couple are living at the same address prior to the wedding.*[3] *In the US, it is now estimated that over 70% of couples live together before marrying.*[4]

Why do people decide to cohabit?

If you ask people who are cohabiting why they are doing so, you get some surprising answers. Many say that they did not have long discussions or make plans to cohabit. They got into a relationship with someone they met and liked, and one thing led to another. It was just easier to live together in the same house. However, this slide into a relationship makes the couple vulnerable to conflicting agendas and painful misunderstandings. One of our friends had a meal with two students, a boy and a girl, who were cohabiting. He asked them how long they planned to stay together. They both answered him at the same time. The girl said, 'For the rest of my life.' The boy said, 'Until the end of term.' They had obviously not discussed the future in any detail.

There are various reasons why couples choose to cohabit before or instead of getting married. Some say that they are 'keeping their options open' or 'just seeing how things go'. In other words, they do not want to make a firm decision about the future. They are not willing to commit themselves fully to the other person and, specifically, they are not willing to commit themselves to the other person in marriage. Others feel emotionally obliged to cohabit because it was expected of them by their partner and any resistance to the idea might seem like an expression of a lack of love.

Often people say that they have chosen to cohabit to find out whether they are suited to each other. Perhaps they think that they cannot make the big commitment of marriage until they know more about the other person. They think that they need to test how well they get on before making a legal commitment, and this means living in the same home and finding out whether they are sexually compatible. If things go well, they may decide to marry. Maybe when a child comes along, then they will give the child increased security by getting married.

Some people feel that marriage is likely to be in some way limiting and see living together as a way of maintaining more independence. Some say they like the freedom of sexual intimacy without serious commitment. Perhaps they like the thought of moving from one partner to another when they feel bored or unfulfilled by their current relationship, or the ability to move because of work. They think that they can do this without any damage to themselves or their partners.

People who have experienced breakdown in their own family may feel anxious about committing to marriage. They fear that they too might be unable to sustain the commitment of marriage and think that cohabitation will remove the potential need to divorce.

Sometimes couples cohabit for financial reasons. They think that because they cannot afford a house and a grand wedding, it would be better to move in together while they save up their money. They might think it would be cheaper to live together, rather than separately.

Some older couples cohabit because they are lonely and want companionship but do not want the commitment of marrying, perhaps for the second time, because their previous spouse has died.

What makes marriage distinct and special?

Marriage is different from cohabitation because it involves promises or vows made in front of witnesses. We read in the book of Genesis, 'a man leaves his father and mother and is united to his wife, and they become one flesh' (Genesis 2:24, NIVUK). This describes how God brought Adam and Eve together as husband and wife and set up the pattern for all future marriages. The promises of marriage express a commitment by a couple to God's design.

These promises or vows are recognised by the law of the land. At a wedding, there must be at least two witnesses present to hear the vows, as well as a person authorised to register the marriage and issue the marriage certificate. Most people invite a much larger group of witnesses to their wedding, usually their family and close friends.

Legally, the couple only have to promise that they are **allowed** to marry and that they **choose** to take each other to be husband and wife.[5] However, in most weddings the bride and bridegroom make a series of profound promises to each other:[6]

- The couple promise to love each other *exclusively*. It is legally possible to marry only one person (though some are now challenging this). But more than that, by promising to forsake all others, they are declaring that they will not let anyone else compete for their romantic and sexual attention.

- The couple also promise to love each other *unconditionally* ('for better, for worse, for richer, for poorer, in sickness and in health'). How special this is! It means that however difficult the circumstances of life might be, they are going to stand by each other faithfully.

- The couple also promise to love each other *forever* ('till death us do part'). Only death may separate those whom God has joined together. God designed marriage to be something that is permanent and blessed because of this. Jesus warns in Matthew 19:6: 'What therefore God has joined together, let not man separate.'

Do promises matter?

In recent years, the progressive liberalisation of divorce laws has made it much easier to break the promises of marriage.

Most recently, in April 2022, the law changed significantly in England and Wales to introduce 'no fault' divorce, which means that a couple can now get divorced solely on the basis that the marriage has broken down, without needing to cite one of the reasons for divorce that were previously required.[7] It is tempting to think that promises do not matter if the law allows us to break them. But is this true? We need to think further about the nature of a promise.

A promise is made before God, whether a person acknowledges that or not. A broken promise involves sinning against God. 'If a man vows a vow to the Lord… he shall not break his word. He shall do according to all that proceeds out of his mouth' (Numbers 30:2).

For this reason, it is essential that when someone plans to make a promise, they consider carefully what they are undertaking. Once the promise is made, they must do everything in their power to keep it. A promise, however big or small, should be made with care and kept with care. God requires us to keep a promise even when it hurts (Psalm 15:4).[8]

There is a motto on the coat of arms of the London Stock Exchange: 'My word is my bond.' In other words, 'When I do business with you, I will keep my promise.' A promise allows others to make plans that depend on it. It is this principle that has allowed the London Stock Exchange to flourish over the last 200 years.

The Coat of Arms of the Stock Exchange: My word is my bond.[9]

The marriage vows of the traditional wedding service are big promises of committed love before God and before witnesses. These promises are legally binding. The couple's attitude to their vows radically affects the way they view their relationship and how they behave. The vows bring reward and security.

The greatest of commitments in life often brings the greatest reward. The marriage vows allow the couple and others to plan their lives depending on them. These plans might include setting up home, helping each other when they are sick, and providing a secure environment to bring up children. The cohabiting couple has made no public promises and so lack the same foundation on which to build their lives and family.

Romantic love is a feeling and feelings can change, but marriage is a commitment. Such a commitment helps sustain the marriage through difficult times when the feelings of romantic love might not be so strong. Dietrich Bonhoeffer, a German theologian in the Second World War, reminds us that in those times, 'It is not your love that upholds marriage, but… it is marriage that upholds your love.'[10]

Sadly, changes in the laws of our country over the last 20 years have undermined marriage. Civil partnerships, sometimes called domestic partnerships in the US, for either same-sex or opposite-sex couples are legally registered relationships, but without the need for vows or promises.[11] They confer very similar legal and financial rights on couples, which makes them look like marriage, despite the lower level of commitment. Furthermore, the UK Government has removed some of the financial and legal advantages of marriage, and, as we have seen, made it increasingly easy to divorce.[12] All these changes can make marriage look more like cohabitation.

For these reasons, some people dismiss marriage as unnecessary, even 'just a piece of paper'. Nevertheless, marriage remains distinctive and special because it has been designed by God. This pattern has been present from the very beginning of human history, even in societies that do not recognise God as its designer. Marriage has been the basis of family life, and families the basis for stable societies, all over the world.

What is wrong with cohabitation?

Looking from the outside, it might seem from a practical perspective that the lifestyle of a cohabiting couple is very similar to that of a married couple. They may share a car and a dog, do the shopping and the gardening together, and enjoy going to parties as an 'item'. The only thing that seems to be missing is the wedding ring!

Whatever the outward appearances, we must trust God's word in assessing how a couple should live. Being obedient to God means doing things in the right order. In the account of marriage in Genesis 2:24, sexual union comes after, not before, the union of marriage. A couple's willingness to keep to this order not only honours God and demonstrates trust that his ways are best but also shows true love and respect for each other and builds up the ability to trust each other in the future.

The circumstances in which we experience sexual intimacy are important to God. Sex is his design and he has determined with whom and when it should be experienced. God placed sex within marriage from the beginning (Matthew 19:4–5) and that is where he means it to remain, so that the love of the husband and wife is strengthened and so that they may have children.[13] The Bible is consistently clear from beginning to end that sexual activity of any sort outside marriage is wrong and should be avoided (1 Corinthians 6:18–20 and 7:9).[14] Because there is a level of commitment in cohabitation, it might look more honourable than casual sex, but living in a cohabiting relationship is still wrong before God.

Does cohabitation deliver?

Poor preparation for marriage

Cohabitation is actually a poor preparation for marriage. As we mentioned, some couples think cohabitation is a good way to see if they are suited to each other and can help them decide whether or not they should get married. However, studies have shown that a couple who live together before they get married are actually more likely to split up than a couple who do not.[15] Thinking more deeply, perhaps this is not surprising as marriage involves the total commitment of a husband and wife to each other and is, therefore, not something you can just 'try out'. As long as there is an 'opt-out', it is easy for couples to split up by saying "it isn't working". It can be difficult to change that mindset if it is something that they have grown used to before they committed to marriage. When a married couple work through the difficult patches that arise, it can be very rewarding for them in the long term, and their children are often very grateful that they did. It is this commitment of marriage that gives a married couple the benefit of lifelong companionship and gives children the stability they need as they grow up.

Unstable

Cohabiting relationships often do not last long. Many cohabiting relationships in the UK last for less than two years.[16] The expectation is only slightly longer in the US.[17] In contrast, 58% of UK marriages, and 59% of US marriages last for life.[18]

The instability of most cohabiting relationships affects children as well. Consider these statistics: children born to a cohabiting couple in the UK are approximately three times more likely to see their parents split up by the age of five compared with those who are born to married parents.[19] The figure is similar in the US.[20] In addition, in the UK 93% of all 13- to 15-year-olds who live with both parents, have married parents.[21] In the US, the chances of parents staying together in their children's early teens also remain significantly higher for those who are married.[22]

The above statistics show that sex outside marriage (which often involves cohabitation) leads to the formation of many single-parent families. Today in the UK, there are nearly 3 million single-parent households.[23] In the US there are 11 million and a child is more likely to live without one of their parents in that country than anywhere else in the world.[24] This involves much sadness for the child in seeing their parents split up and can result in many difficulties for the parent who is looking after a child (or children) alone. Sadly, if a parent leaves the family home, their children do not benefit from the 24/7 care and role model of their mother – or, more usually, their father.

Misusing God's gift of sexual intimacy

God designed sexual intimacy to create a deep bond between a husband and wife as they share themselves at the deepest level. A study showed that those who follow God's design by keeping sex for marriage enjoy intimacy more than those who do not.[25] Conversely, the instability of many cohabiting relationships gives rise to a great deal of pain as those who have been so closely bonded go their separate ways. Any further sexual relationship may be clouded by the experiences of the past.

Missing the fertile years

A woman's fertility declines with age (see chart below).[26] Some women who have cohabited for a long time, wanting to be married before having children, may find it harder to conceive if they marry later in life.

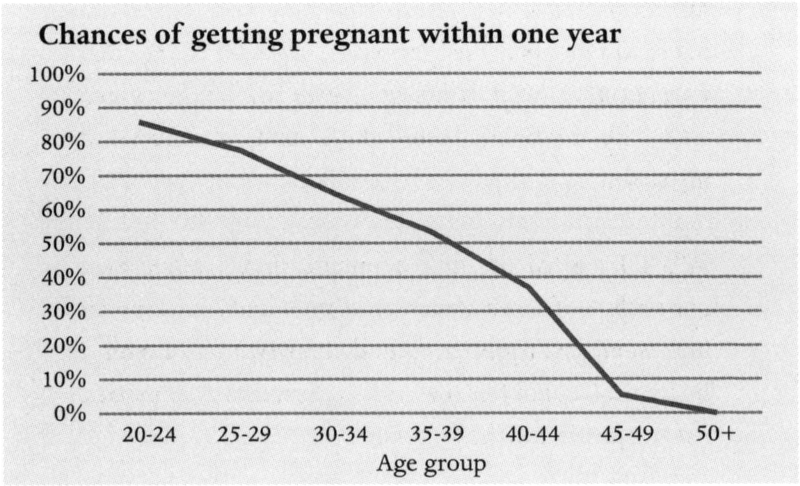

Source of information: https://www.kinderzeit.org/en/fertility-by-age/

Gina's testimony (names changed here and in some of the other testimonies to maintain confidentiality)

Here is the testimony of someone who thought that cohabitation would give her the love and security she was looking for. Ultimately she was disappointed, and discovered that true contentment could only be found in God and living in the way he designed.

I'm called Gina and I was born in Switzerland. I grew up in a Christian home with my three brothers. From when I was small, I was raised with biblical values. As a young girl, I gave my life to the Lord Jesus and followed him until I went to secondary school. The change from primary school to secondary school allowed me to go down a worldly path, which I knowingly chose. At the same time, I often felt very religiously constrained by my father. He spoke very clearly about the direction I had taken. It often made me furious. It was clear to me that I would never want a husband who was so 'black and white' like my father. I rebelled against God and against my parents.

When I started my first apprenticeship, I often went out with my friends, drinking alcohol and searching for love, along with protection and security, from a man. I imagined I would find love as it is depicted in the movies. I strove for the attention of men.

I soon met my boyfriend while going out and, despite warnings from friends, we became a couple. This was the love that I was searching for! Very quickly after we became a couple, I moved in with Tom and we lived together as an unmarried couple.

Everything seemed perfect. I felt comfortable with him and was head over heels in love. It was clear to me that I wanted to marry this man. From the beginning, however, I had a bad feeling about being sexually intimate when we were not married. Sometimes my conscience was bothered more and sometimes less. The biblical values from my childhood never quite left me and I often tried to push them away.

During this time two things happened that made me stop and reflect and it became very clear to me that what I was doing wasn't right. I had two serious car accidents. I can remember that in the second car accident I thought that it was all over because the car flipped onto its roof. About six months after, when we were on holiday visiting my relatives, I came to realise that at some point this relationship would no longer be able to function. However, I continued to live with Tom with conflicting feelings and still believed that I had found a man to love me.

Having lived with Tom for a year, I was on a night out with friends when my mother phoned me. She did not sound happy – actually she sounded very disappointed that I didn't go show up to listen to my older brother preaching but had instead decided to go out.

That was a decisive point in my life. I slowly realised that what I was doing wasn't right. It didn't satisfy me at all. The love that I had searched for wasn't enough. I started going to church and my youth group again. I wanted to bring Tom with me and I spoke with him about the gospel – but he didn't want to hear. The only thing that he was prepared to do was to meet once with the minister of our church. In this meeting, my boyfriend was very clear that he wanted the old Gina back.

It was over a number of days that I implored the Lord to forgive my sins, and I asked him into my life. One day after that while I was at home I called Tom and told him that I was going to live with my brother and his wife. At that moment, I was full of doubt and sorrow but I couldn't stand my sin anymore. Therefore, I packed up my clothes and went to my oldest brother's home for a few months.

Because of my love for Tom and the hope that I still had for our relationship, I didn't stop contact with him. For four months we would regularly meet up. I clung to this relationship like it was a lifeline. We both knew that this couldn't actually function but we continued for four months until Tom ended the relationship. He said to me that he couldn't string it along with me any more.

My world broke apart. I cried a lot. I knew, however, that it was the right decision and that we had no future together. At that time, I didn't think that living together before being married was intrinsically wrong, although the sexual aspect had always given me a bad conscience. Slowly, however, I came to realise that living with him led me into the temptations to which I succumbed. I never had the strength to resist Tom and the time I lived with him created a strong bond between him and me. The continuing consequences of my sins are often painful. I still inwardly struggle five years after the break-up. The old life has left many wounds behind.

Today, I can say that I do not regret stepping away from my old life. The Lord Jesus has shown me through this, however, that my true desire for love couldn't be satisfied in any person in this world. The one who does truly satisfy is God himself and he carries me through all the difficulties. Now, despite my disobedience and rebellious behaviour, God has given me a husband who is a Christian. I do not want to take it for granted that God was and is so gracious to me.

3

Pornography

We live in a world where people have taken God's good gift of sex and used it in ways that God did not intend. God's gift of sex rightly belongs within marriage, where it is given to bless and strengthen the relationship between a husband and wife.

But some people have photographed or made films of sexual acts or nudity. Those pictures are called pornography and are now often seen on the internet. Unfortunately, in our culture, especially because of the internet, there is now more of this material than ever before. You can even come across it without meaning to and it may be that friends may try to show you pictures which you should not and do not want to see.

Initial response

If you come across pornographic material for the first time, it can be very upsetting. This feeling of being upset is a God-given response, rather like suddenly discovering that you are trespassing on someone else's land. Your response may be, and should be, to run away from it, close the website down, or tell your friend that you do not want to see the pictures, and then make every effort to avoid it in the future.

But you may have a different reaction: that of curiosity. It may all seem strange, but at the same time interesting and attractive, and you feel that you would like to know more – just as the trespasser may be tempted to see what the house and garden are like. Be very careful about this response because curiosity is often used by the devil to draw people into sin. It is likely that it was curiosity that drew Eve to the fruit of the one tree from which she was forbidden to eat. Our response to things that are wrong should always be to run, rather than to linger and sin.

It is possible that seeing pornographic images may feel good to you. In this case, we must remember that the forbidden fruit was exceedingly attractive to Eve. She saw it was 'good for food and pleasing to the eye, and also desirable for gaining wisdom' (Genesis 3:6 NIVUK). You may be attracted to the excitement of discovering secret knowledge about a person or finding out more about sex. But remember that just because something feels good at the time, it does not mean that it is right, and, as we will explain later, it may lead to bitter feelings of guilt and regret. It is important to learn about sex in the right way, probably from your parents, and to constantly keep in mind that God designed it as a special gift only to be used in the right context of marriage.

Secrecy

The ability to hide the use of pornography makes it particularly dangerous. When we meet and relate to others, people see us and know what we are doing and so we are accountable. Interaction with a computer is much easier to hide from others, even our parents.

Most young people who look at pornography do it in secret and, if challenged, lie about what they are doing. Why is this? If they are honest, they would probably admit that they know that they are doing something wrong, feel ashamed and want to hide it from others. Jesus warned us that people will try to hide sinful actions: 'For everyone who does wicked things hates the light and does not come to the light, lest his works should be exposed' (John 3:20).

Even if a person succeeds in hiding their actions from other people, they cannot hide them from God. He knows everything – all that we say and do. There is no escape from our accountability to God.

What is wrong with pornography?

It is a sin

Sex can rightly be described as a holy act. 'Holy' describes something specially designed and set apart by God. Sex is set apart by our holy God for the holy institution of marriage. We can be sure of this because God has given us a commandment, 'You shall not commit adultery' (Exodus 20:14), which requires that sexual intimacy is kept for marriage and only for marriage.

Sexual intimacy is the closest form of physical relationship that any two people can experience. It is sometimes referred to as 'making love' because it is a special and close way that a husband and wife show that they love each other. God intends that the closest form of physical intimacy is preserved for the most committed of all relationships – that of marriage.

Pornography provokes sexual desire and arousal towards someone who is not your wife or husband. It takes sex outside of the God-given context of marriage. In this way it causes someone to sin by breaking God's law. It damages or profanes something holy. The Bible refers to these wrong desires as 'lusts' (for example, Matthew 5:28).

You might have been thinking that sex always needs to involve another person, so looking at pornography is not really breaking the command to keep sex for marriage. However, God wants us to have pure *thoughts* as well as *actions*. Jesus made it clear that it is wrong to think sexual thoughts and have sexual desires towards someone who is not your husband or wife: 'You have heard that it was said, "You shall not commit adultery." But I say to you that everyone who looks at a woman with lustful intent has already committed adultery with her in his heart' (Matthew 5:27–28).

Often the use of pornography is accompanied by

self-stimulation, otherwise known as masturbation. Masturbation is wrong and should be avoided (you can read more using the QR code below).[1]

Distorted relationships

God designed sex for the relationship of marriage, but with pornography, there is *no relationship* – only interaction with an image or video. There is no commitment and no responsibility to look after, care for and be faithful to another person. Pornography is *unrealistic* because it distorts what real, loving relationships should be like.

It is also unrealistic because it is entirely visual – it's all about what people look like. In contrast, if you want a real relationship, it is most important to consider a person's character, personality and attitudes. For these reasons, images on a screen are unrewarding and dangerous. They will never give the lasting fulfilment of companionship and family life.

Unloving

Using pornography is not loving. There is no love shared. Actually, the opposite is true – the use of pornography is very selfish. It makes sexual experience all about the person using it. This is called 'self-gratification'. There is no thought about the happiness or needs of someone else.

What was designed by God to be an expression of love in a marriage is being abused in a loveless and uncommitted experience that leaves feelings of emptiness, loneliness and guilt.

Using pornography also shows an unloving attitude towards the people depicted in it, because looking at them in this way objectifies them (meaning that they are treated as something only to provide enjoyment for others, rather than as people in their own right), depriving them of the dignity and respect they deserve as human beings who are made in the image of God. Many people who appear in pornographic films and images are also the victims of crime: they are often abused or mistreated by the content creators and may even become the victims of trafficking and modern slavery. Anyone who views pornographic material is supporting and encouraging this mistreatment.

Not modest

Viewing pornography involves looking at things that are meant by God to be hidden. There are parts of our body that Paul refers to as 'unpresentable' (1 Corinthians 12:23).[2] These are parts which we normally keep private by covering them with clothes. The verse tells us that we need to treat these parts with special modesty or respect. If you are in any doubt, think how it would feel if you had to walk to school with no clothes on. Apart from being very cold, you would also feel intensely embarrassed. God has given us an instinct to keep these 'private parts' private – away from the sight of others except in very special circumstances, such as when we need to be examined by a doctor.

Breaking the law

Sometimes people send or are asked to send sexually explicit messages, images or videos to others (this is sometimes called 'sexting'). It is very risky behaviour which puts them in a vulnerable position. Such messages can easily be widely distributed beyond the initial recipient, and if the image goes online it can be very hard to get it taken down.

As well as being wrong and unloving, sexting is also illegal. It is an offence to create, possess, share or show 'indecent' images of under-18s. Children and young people who share nudes or semi-nudes of themselves or their friends (even if created and shared with consent) are breaking the law.[3] This is a serious safeguarding issue, and under certain circumstances it could result in a caution or conviction, which could have damaging implications for your future. It is also against the law to look at pornography or distribute it to anyone under 18.

Using pornography is very damaging

It spoils our relationship with God

For Christians, our relationship with God is the most precious of all relationships. We are commanded by God to love him with all our heart and with all our soul and with all our mind (Matthew 22:37).[4] We show our love for God by obeying his commandments. Sin always damages our relationship with God because sin is, by definition, the very opposite of his nature and involves rejection of his authority. Ongoing and deliberate sin in our lives stops us from wanting to read the Bible, pray and serve God.

It disturbs the mind and damages the soul

We have mentioned that the use of pornography is often accompanied by feelings of guilt and regret. There is a sense of guilt when we know we have done something wrong before God, and regret because we wish that we had not done something wrong. We might also fear being found out.

It also leaves lasting images in the mind which are very hard to remove. Someone observed that it was so much easier to get rid of their smartphone than the images that they had seen on it. These memories can affect friendships and future marriage relationships.

Using pornography stirs up sexual feelings at the wrong time. God intends that you wait for these feelings until you are ready for marriage.

Looking at pornographic images can become a selfish preoccupation, and many will testify that it causes them to spend less and less time with those who care about them, and more time alone. It can become addictive. Many people who have looked at pornography say that as time went on, they felt the need to look at more and more extreme images. The effects of pornography on the brain can be very similar to the use of addictive drugs. It can become harder and harder to stop watching pornography, even if it is obvious that it is having a bad effect on you.

It affects our relationship with others

Although many people in our society don't believe this, viewing pornography is a loveless and selfish pursuit and hardens our hearts toward others. Pornography crudely cuts up a person, making them an object for our selfish entertainment which is far separated from the reality of the person – their lives, thoughts, needs and situation and how we relate to them. Once our mind gets used to this, it can affect all kinds of relationships including close friendships.

It damages marriage

We have already explained how God protects marriage by requiring that sexual intimacy is kept as a gift of love between a husband and wife (Exodus 20:14 and 1 Corinthians 7:4).[5] If we choose to disregard God's protective laws by experiencing sex casually and selfishly, this not only wastes the gift of sex on the wrong person and in the wrong context, but also damages marriage.

Looking at pornographic images can damage marriage long before you actually get married by distorting the way that you think about marriage and how you view someone you might marry. Once married, viewing pornography is being sexually unfaithful to your wife or husband and can rightly be called mental adultery. It will cause unhappiness, jealousy and insecurity. Tragically, many couples can tell you about the way that pornography has badly affected their marriages.

What to do

Like other sins, viewing pornography starts in the heart, from where all sinful thoughts and desires arise. Make a firm decision before God that you will do everything with his mighty help to avoid this sin that so easily entangles many young people in a horrible net of pain and misery. Job made such a resolution and called this 'making a covenant with his eyes' (Job 31:1).[6]

Take practical steps to avoid temptation

When you make a firm decision to turn away from or avoid pornography, God expects you to back it up with all practical arrangements that will help you to be obedient in this area. Otherwise you may let Satan get a foothold on you again. These arrangements might include:

- Making sure you have a high-level filter on all your internet access.
- Using the internet in areas of the home where you are accountable to your parents.
- Asking your parents to use internet accountability software, such as Covenant Eyes, so that they are aware of all the sites that you are accessing.

- Being especially careful when searching for photos or videos, because even with the use of a high-level filter, it is still possible to come across pornographic material by mistake.

If you have ever been tempted in this area, take radical action. Tell someone you trust, which may be your parents. Because they love you, your parents will want to help you stop looking at such images because they recognise what a bad effect it can have on you both now and in the future. In Matthew 5:29–30, Jesus reminds us of the seriousness of sin. He says it would be better to lose part of your body than face eternal punishment because you have used it to sin.[7] You might conclude that it is better to deny yourself unsupervised access to the internet than risk facing God's judgment for using it sinfully.

You might have heard, for example in a PSHE or Sex Ed lesson or from an information website, that looking at pornography 'just a bit', or using it occasionally, is alright – that it can be fun, or even helpful in some way. This is not true. For many of the reasons already mentioned in this chapter, getting involved with pornography in any way is wrong – it is harmful both to those who use it and those who feature in it, and most of all it harms our relationship with God. As with other temptations, if we give in to it just a small amount, we can end up being drawn further and further into sin because it can never satisfy us.

What to do if you have seen things that you should not

This may not be your fault. It may have been accidental, or it may not have been your fault initially because you were shown something by someone else and you were drawn in by curiosity. Or you may have fallen fully to temptation. If you are in any doubt or have a sense of guilt, bring these matters before God and ask him to forgive you for any way that you have sinned. He is able and willing to separate our sins from us 'as far as the east is from the west' (Psalm 103:12).

God's grace provides us with the opportunity for a fresh start, no matter what we have done, so we can put aside the guilt of the past and look forward to serving him in the future. Ask God for his strength to be obedient in the future and to clear wrong things from your mind. He offers to lead you 'in paths of righteousness for his name's sake' (Psalm 23:3).

Testimony of someone who used pornography

Paul writes about his experience of using pornography:

> *I first saw pornography when I was twelve years old. One of my friends had a magazine on the back of the school bus which had pictures of naked women in it. I was shocked and felt sick, but I couldn't look away. Growing up in a Christian family I knew that pornography was sinful, but the women were beautiful and part of me really enjoyed looking at them. As I got off the bus I felt*

ashamed and worried that I would get into trouble, so I didn't tell anyone what had happened.

Over the next few years, I slowly became addicted to pornography. It was free, easily accessible on the internet, and it seemed like it didn't hurt anyone. Shame and fear of the consequences kept me from telling anyone, and besides, if I was honest with myself, I wanted to look at it. When people asked me about porn or sexual temptation, I'd either say something vague like, 'I struggle from time to time, but nothing too serious,' or I'd just flat-out lie. But from my late teens on I used internet porn almost every day.

I became a Christian aged 15 but I spent a lot of my time feeling really miserable. 'Jesus must be so disappointed with me,' I thought. 'He can't love me when I'm living like this.' I constantly told myself, 'that was the last time I'll ever look at that.' But then, soon enough, I'd do it again. I was trapped. 'I can't tell anyone,' I thought. 'If I do, it will be so embarrassing and I'll be in so much trouble.' As I got older, the reasons not to tell people only got bigger. I got involved in Christian ministry. I started dating a beautiful girl, who then became my fiancée, and then my wife. I was appointed trainee minister at a large church. My wife became pregnant with our first child. And all the time I was thinking, 'You can't tell. You have to stop this. I can't stop this.' It was awful.

Satan does his best work when sin is kept hidden. He tells you that confessing will hurt too much and your life will be destroyed. He tells you that Jesus hates you, and that you should hate yourself. He tells you that the only thing that will make you feel better is looking at porn. And I listened to him, mainly because I loved porn and wanted an excuse to keep watching it.

But Satan is a liar. Jesus didn't hate me. He loved me more than I could understand. The cross assures me of that. And so, He gave me three gifts of grace.

First, he allowed my life to be utterly miserable. He wasn't going to let me think that porn was the path to joy. Porn wrecked everything, and I got to the point where I couldn't go on. He disciplined me so that I would turn back to him.

Second, he gave me the courage to confess. I'm not going to lie, it was awful. I will never forget how painful those conversations with my wife and my church were. Seeing and experiencing the consequences of my sin was horrible. But Jesus helped me get through it and protected both my wife and me as the world felt like it was falling apart.

And third, he granted me the power to change. I began to experience the power of the Holy Spirit like never before. I stopped looking at pornography. I stopped lying about what I had been doing. And I began to enjoy closer relationships with God and other people.

1 John 1:7 (NIVUK) says, 'if we walk in the light, as he is in the light, we have fellowship with one another, and the blood of Jesus, his Son, purifies us from all sin.'

Pornography keeps us hiding in the darkness, separates us from other people, and allows sin to grow. But when we confess (walk in the light), we connect with other people (fellowship), and Jesus changes us (purifies us from all sin).

I know this verse is true because I have lived it. It can be true for you, too. You are not too far gone for Jesus. He can fix the mess you have made. But you have to stop hiding and walk in the light.

Be brave. Trust Jesus. He will not let you down.

4

Homosexuality

As you go through puberty, your body and mind undergo big changes which come about through hormones in your blood. These changes can occur quickly over a short space of time and can be quite bewildering. You are likely to experience a lot of new feelings including those of sexual attraction, usually towards the opposite sex. This is part of God's design. He gives these feelings so that one day, you may meet someone you want to marry and have a family with. However, it is not unusual for a teenager to become very close to a friend of the same sex (often slightly older), and occasionally this may involve strong feelings for them. These feelings can be confusing. However, such feelings are often short-lived and do not mean that those who experience them will be attracted to those of the same sex in the long term. Young people need to be very careful about labelling themselves at this stage (or any other stage) of their lives. For a few people, same-sex attraction is something that they continue to or start to experience when they get older, but the majority of people identify as heterosexual in adulthood.[1]

Nowadays, men who are attracted to other men are usually referred to as gay, and women attracted to other women are referred to as lesbian. There are also some people who are attracted to both sexes, and they are often referred to as bisexual. You may also hear terms such as homosexual, pansexual, queer or questioning – all of which may relate to a person who experiences attraction to the same sex. You have probably seen the acronym LGBTQ used when referring to people who experience same-sex attraction. 'L' stands for lesbian, 'G' for gay and 'B' for bisexual. The 'T' stands for transgender – this is different from same-sex attraction and is discussed in chapter 5, *Gender Identity*. 'Q' stands for queer or questioning, referring to those who say that they are still exploring their sexuality.

Important to think clearly and biblically

Christians need to know what the Bible teaches about same-sex attraction and homosexual practice. There are several reasons why it is important to develop a clear Christian understanding on this issue.

First, it is often claimed as a moral right that people, hetero- or homosexual, should be allowed to express their sexual desires in whatever way they wish, providing both parties are able to give consent. Those who say that homosexuality is wrong are often accused of doing wrong themselves: it is said that they are showing discrimination, or even hatred, against those who practise homosexuality. They are sometimes described as 'homophobic'.

Second, the state has largely accepted a pro-homosexual perspective. Sixty years ago, homosexual activity was illegal. Now it has been affirmed in law. In 2004, a law was passed that created a legally recognised same-sex relationship called a civil partnership and then in 2013 a law was passed allowing same-sex couples to marry (according to a legal, rather than biblical, definition of marriage). Same-sex marriage may have redefined marriage according to the *law*, but the true nature of marriage cannot be changed. In line with many international bodies such as the United Nations, the UK Government now promotes homosexual rights. Homosexuality is normalised and even celebrated in some schools and spoken about by many politicians in supportive terms. Because homosexuality is now legally accepted and promoted, many in our society have become convinced that it is morally acceptable.

Third, churches have often not been clear about, or have undermined, what the Bible says on the subject. Some claim that there is nothing wrong with homosexual activity. Others claim that homosexual activity is wrong but that there is no need to guard our hearts and minds against same-sex attraction. Therefore, there is much confusion among Christians in this country.

Fourth, people with same-sex attraction have sometimes been treated badly, both by the church and by society in general.

So, in the midst of all this confusion and pressure, it is very important to turn to the authority of God's word in the Bible to gain a God-centred perspective.

The goodness of the original design

God designed the institution of marriage. The first marriage is described in the second chapter of Genesis and is between a man and a woman. We know that God intends their marriage to be a model for all future marriages because its description is followed by a generalisation: 'That is why a man leaves his father and mother and is united to his wife, and they become one flesh' (Genesis 2:24, NIVUK). One key aspect of the design was that marriage should be between a man and a woman, and not between two men or two women. This marriage occurred before the Fall, so we can be certain that it is part of God's perfect design for men and women, and we can be sure that this principle applies for all time because it is affirmed in the rest of the Bible.

There are many obvious practical and scientific reasons why marriage is rightly between a man and a woman and not between those of the same sex. Although men and women are equal, they are also designed by God to be very different – both in body and mind – in order that they can work in a complementary way in marriage.

Physically, men and women are very different for a purpose. This is perhaps most obvious with regard to the sex organs. During sexual intimacy, described in the Bible as the two 'becoming one flesh', they fit together perfectly. As a result of sexual intimacy, the sperm of the man may fuse with the egg of the woman to form new life in the woman's womb. This enables a married couple to have a family as God designed it. A sperm cannot fuse with a sperm or an egg with an egg. Two men or two women cannot have children naturally.

But the differences are not limited to the physical body. The minds of men and women work differently and tend to a different range of desires, emotions and interests. The different strengths and qualities of their bodies and minds allow the husband and wife to work together to fulfil different roles and responsibilities in marriage for the good of each other.

In addition, the Bible explains that the 'one flesh' unity in the relationship of marriage is a picture of the greater spiritual relationship between Jesus Christ and his church (Ephesians 5:31–32). (We will talk more about this in chapter 9). Same-sex union therefore distorts this precious relationship and thereby the heart of the gospel message.

Sin affects how men and women relate

At the Fall, the world was turned upside down when Satan deceived Adam and Eve and they ate the fruit which God had forbidden them to eat. Through this disobedience, sin came into the world and both men and women started to have thoughts and temptations that they were never designed to experience. One of these is that some men and women, for a variety of reasons, are sexually attracted to those of the same sex.

We learn about how men and women should act in the fallen world through the Ten Commandments. These laws were given by God to reflect his holy nature and serve to direct us as to how we should relate to God and to other people. The Ten Commandments are often called the *moral law* because they inform us what is right and what is wrong. The law concerning marriage and sexual intimacy is the seventh commandment which reads: 'You shall not commit adultery' (Exodus 20:14). Simply put, this means: 'keep sex for your husband or wife in marriage'.

God provides a detailed explanation of this commandment in Leviticus 18:22: 'Do not have sexual relations with a man as one does with a woman; that is detestable' (NIVUK). That is strong language and reveals that homosexual acts are an offence to God. It is also a reminder to us more generally that we are only to experience the gift of sexual intimacy in a way that pleases God. Homosexual acts destroy God's good and right design for sexual intimacy and so threaten his holy institution of marriage.

Some people have said that this verse is not relevant, noting that some of the Old Testament commands (for example, not shaving the sides of a man's beard) are ceremonial laws that have been fulfilled with Christ's coming. However, we can be sure this commandment against homosexuality still stands by turning to several clear verses in the New Testament.

It is sometimes said that Jesus teaches nothing about homosexuality. But this is a misunderstanding. In Matthew 19:4–5, he clearly repeats Genesis 2:24 and so affirms that marriage is to be between a man and a woman.[2]

In his letter to the church at Rome, the Apostle Paul warns them that because some people had failed to thank God for his goodness and had turned from God to worship idols, God removed his restraining influence from them and allowed them to follow their own sinful desires. One result was that both men and women were having sex with same-sex partners. He wrote: 'Because of this, God gave them over to shameful lusts. Even their women exchanged natural sexual relations for unnatural ones. In the same way the men also abandoned natural relations with women and were inflamed with lust for one another' (Romans 1:26–27a, NIVUK).

Paul describes such homosexual acts as 'unnatural', meaning that they go against God's original design. He describes those involved being subject to 'shameful lusts', meaning desires that dishonour God. Both descriptions make it quite clear that giving way to homosexual desires and so engaging in homosexual activity is wrong.

The good news of forgiveness

But to anyone who has sinned in this area, God stands

ready to forgive. In his letter to the church at Corinth, the Apostle Paul reminds them that some of them had once lived a life of sexual immorality. He includes adulterers and homosexuals in the list of wrongdoers:

> *Or do you not know that the unrighteous will not inherit the kingdom of God? Do not be deceived: neither the sexually immoral, nor idolaters, nor adulterers, nor men who practice homosexuality, nor thieves, nor the greedy, nor drunkards, nor revilers, nor swindlers will inherit the kingdom of God. And such were some of you. But you were washed, you were sanctified, you were justified in the name of the Lord Jesus Christ and by the Spirit of our God.* (1 Corinthians 6:9–11)

Note Paul's striking comment, 'such were some of you' (verse 11). This shows us that there were people living in Corinth who used to be actively homosexual, but who had recognised it as a sin and had turned from it to receive forgiveness from God.

Whatever temptations we have given into, if we give our lives fully to Jesus, with the help of the Holy Spirit, we can overcome any sin and change our behaviours and thoughts. This gives hope to anyone today who has been involved in homosexual activity, that they too can be transformed by God's love.

We conclude from the Bible that homosexual activity is sinful. But this does not mean that Christians hate people who are homosexual (as has sometimes been suggested). We are all sinners in need of forgiveness through the sacrifice of the Lord Jesus Christ on the cross. We should welcome everyone into our churches, show people God's love and faithfully teach God's word.

Is there anything wrong with same-sex attraction?

It is clear from the Bible that *acting* on same-sex attraction is wrong. But is simply *being sexually attracted* to someone of the same sex wrong? We have already explained that such feelings go against God's natural designs and are a result of the fallen world in rebellion against God. Indeed, in the above passage from Romans 1 such desires are described as 'shameful'. But are they sinful in themselves if they do not lead to homosexual activity? If someone feels that they can avoid same-sex activity, should they be content to grow comfortable with their same-sex attraction?

Many believers who experience same-sex attraction describe how these feelings bubble up without any deliberate encouragement and are often wrapped up with their past experiences. Frustrating and recurring as these experiences might be, the Bible is clear that such desires are to be resisted.

From one perspective, same-sex attraction is no different in character from a married man being attracted to a woman who is not his wife. He must not linger thinking or fantasising about the woman, nor, most serious of all, act upon his desires. God has made it clear that any sex with, or sexual thoughts about, someone who you are not married to is wrong, whatever their sex. So we need to turn to God in repentance and, when these thoughts occur, we need to take steps, in his strength, to stamp them out and focus our minds on being obedient to Christ (2 Corinthians 10:5).[3]

One practical way to pursue obedience is to avoid the situations that tempt us, whether that is when we find ourselves alone, when we watch certain TV shows or read certain books, or when we are with others who are discussing who they 'like'. All of us experience different sources of temptation. The sensible approach is to identify them and keep away from them. Just as we considered in the chapter on pornography, it might be difficult to sacrifice things we enjoy, but we know that it is worthwhile so that we can remain faithful to God (Matthew 5:29–30). Those resisting the temptation of same-sex attraction can go to God for all spiritual help – especially through prayer, reading the Bible and thinking about what it says.

This process of battling against wrong desires affects all Christians in one form or other. The activity of turning away from sinful desires is part of our growth in holiness called sanctification. There is an important difference between *justification* (coming to faith and being made right before God), which is all of God's work and none of ours, and *sanctification* (our growth in holiness during our Christian life) which can be described as 'co-operative'. In Romans 6:11–12 the Apostle Paul tells Christians not to allow sin to control their bodies. We co-operate or work hand-in-hand with God – he gives us spiritual help by his Holy Spirit, and we determine to live in obedience to him, seeking to glorify him in our lives (see, for example, Philippians 3:14).[4]

Just because a person continues to experience same-sex attraction, this should not make them doubt that they are saved. On the contrary, they are only battling against such desires because they *are* saved, and God is pleased with all their efforts to turn away from sin and grow in godliness.

Practical points

Helping others who experience same-sex attraction

If you haven't already, sooner or later you are likely to meet those who say that they experience same-sex attraction.

There are various reasons why this might be the case. They might be going through the challenges of puberty and are not really sure what they feel. They may have had some thoughts this way and are wondering why. They might be lonely and want to identify with a group who claim similar things.

Whatever the reason, in our current culture, they are likely to be surrounded by people who encourage them in what they feel. Knowing what you know about God's ways, you may be able to give them some gentle help. How you speak the truth in love (Ephesians 4:15) is challenging. As you think about how to do this, it is important to bring the situation before God in prayer, asking the Lord to help your friend as well as helping you to be faithful to his word. Remember that love is not arrogant or rude (1 Corinthians 13:4–5), so raise the matter with great sensitivity and only with a humble and gentle spirit.

There are many others who can help those with unwanted same-sex attraction. Sometimes young people fear talking to their parents, but many parents will be good listeners and guides in such circumstances. If the young person is a Christian, they may find it helpful to talk to their minister or an older Christian whom they respect and trust.

Standing firm

Holding a biblical view of homosexuality (and other matters covered in this book) can make us very unpopular nowadays. You may be accused wrongly of being homophobic. There will be times to keep your views to yourself, especially if you sense that you face a trick question. But there are also times when you may need to take a stand and make your views clear.

For example, your school might decide to hold a Pride event (a rally that affirms those who identify as homosexual or transgender) and a friend invites you along. Think and pray hard before you answer. You will need to decline the invitation politely – you may simply say, 'No thank you,' as you would if someone invited you to a party you didn't want to go to. Maybe you will have the opportunity to explain your decision to your friend. As you face situations like these, pray for courage to be distinctively Christian, for great wisdom, and for loving compassion for those who don't know God.

Sarah's testimony

An increasing number of people who have been involved in homosexual activity are becoming Christians and experiencing the transforming power of God's love. Here is one person's story:

> *I was brought up in church. My parents, while both active in the church, were in a volatile relationship; my father was an angry man and many of my childhood memories are of fear. As a teenager I struggled with same-sex attraction. I was too scared to tell anyone that I had sexual feelings towards other girls. I thought that God would not understand – that he would be angry and unforgiving. I didn't ever contemplate how my sexuality could fit in with a Christian faith, because I had already made my mind up that no one would understand my feelings, least of all God.*
>
> *Outside of church I was a really sporty teenager. I loved playing any kind of sport and was soon playing for older teams and in women's sport clubs. That was where I first met people who were living in same-sex relationships and this made me think more about the feelings I was experiencing. It wasn't long before I started acting on my same-sex attraction and when I moved away from home as a student to Nottingham, I started going to gay pubs and clubs and had a number of relationships with women.*

I didn't go to church any more. I had run away from God and was a lesbian for many years. But one day God spoke to me and I realised that I had got it wrong: God did love me, and he was more than enough to help me live my life in the way he wanted me to. What was so amazing was that I wasn't looking for God to be a part of my life, but he had clearly never turned his back on me and was asking me to think about him again. After 30 years of being away from church, one Sunday morning in 2014, I walked into my local church searching for something. That was the start of a difficult but amazing journey.

When I started going back to church, I was listening to a lot of different voices. I was watching YouTube videos, reading books and articles, and surfing the internet looking at many different websites which told me lots of conflicting information about same-sex attraction and Christianity. The one thing I didn't do straight away was talk to God about my feelings. I didn't read the Bible and then ask God what his word meant for me. I was actually obsessed with getting the opinions of other humans and didn't place any importance on asking God about what he thought. It wasn't until I was challenged in church by a preacher who asked, 'Have you opened every door of your heart to Jesus?' that I realised the importance of asking God about what he thought about that area of my life. That is when I realised how much God loved me, how he wanted the best for me, and how he would equip me, even though it seemed really scary and hard to change my sexual identity.

Since the day I gave my life to Jesus and surrendered my same-sex attraction to him, my life has changed for the better. He has helped me to live in obedience to his word, and over time he has changed how I feel, and I am no longer same-sex attracted. God has been amazing, and he will be amazing towards anyone who makes sacrifices within their own life because of their love for him.

I know how confusing it is to listen to all the different voices of the world. I also know how rewarding it is when you realise that it doesn't matter what the world says, and you finally listen to what God says. Trust in God and his word tells us that he will honour you. 'Those who honour me I will honour' (1 Samuel 2:30).

5

Gender identity

You might be wondering why gender identity has become such a big issue over the last few years. Much of this comes from the work of philosophers who have attacked the idea that gender identity is binary (composed of two) and, through this, have sought to destroy the concept of heterosexuality (sexual attraction only to people of the opposite sex).[1] This has led to the idea that *any* sexual behaviour should be socially and legally acceptable. This kind of thinking has opened the door to a lot of confusion in our culture. We hope that this chapter will help you think clearly about some of the challenges and questions raised by this confusion.

You may have heard of people saying that they have changed their sex. This may stir up the following questions in your mind: Can a person really change their sex? What does God think about someone who tries to do so? How do we respond to such a person in a loving way that honours God?

Let us begin to answer these questions by looking at what the Bible says about being male and female.

Made in God's image – male and female

When God created the world, he made all human beings 'in his own image' (Genesis 1:27). For this reason, both men and women are equally valuable to God. They also have many similarities. For example, both have a God-given conscience to distinguish right from wrong, and both have the capacity to relate to God.

God also created human beings to be male or female. 'So God created man in his own image, in the image of God he created him; male and female he created them' (Genesis 1:27). Jesus repeated this truth in Mark 10:6, 'But from the beginning of creation, "God made them male and female."' God has made men and women distinct and different. Our maleness or femaleness is sometimes called our 'sex' (but see below for a detailed discussion of the words 'sex' and 'gender').

We see several things from these verses:

1. Our sex is *God-given*. We did not choose whether we were a boy or girl – God did. The Bible describes God's creation of mankind as 'very good'. God chose us to be male or female for our benefit. It is a gift that will be full of God's blessing if we accept it and use it wisely. While some claim that our sex is assigned

at a pregnancy scan or at birth, it is actually determined at conception when an egg is fertilised by a sperm carrying either a single X chromosome or a single Y chromosome.

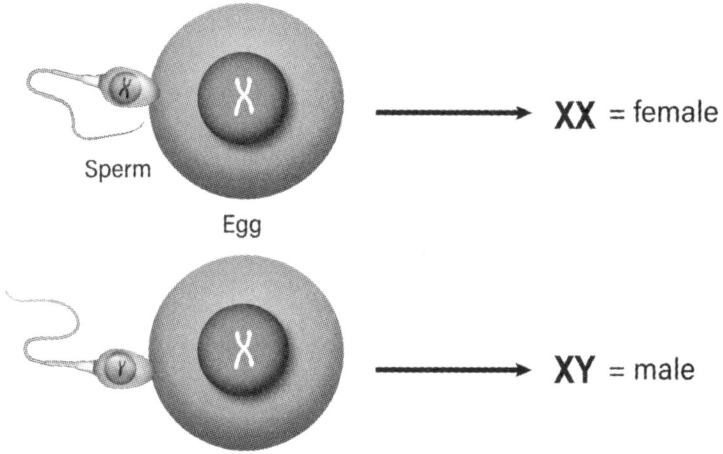

2. Our sex is *fixed*. Our sex is an essential part of us which cannot be changed. However hard we try we cannot become male when we have been created female, or female when we have been made male. All the cells of our body carry either XX (female) or XY (male) sex chromosomes. (The exception to this is in a very few people with one of the rare 'intersex' conditions.)[2]

3. As with all of God's designs, the creation of men and women has *a good purpose*. We get a hint

of this purpose by noting the verse immediately after God's creation of male and female. He commands mankind to 'be fruitful and multiply' (Genesis 1:28). God created men and women so that, among other things, they might marry, have children and populate the world.

Men and women are different

In order that men and women could fulfil this good purpose, God has made men and women not only equal, but different. These differences involve their bodies and their minds – how they feel and what they think.

The differences in the body are obvious from our earliest moments. It is possible to find out the sex of an unborn child in the mother's womb by ultrasound from only 12 weeks into a pregnancy. After birth the differences are obvious to anybody who changes a nappy! The differences become even more marked as a child goes through puberty.

The physical differences are not just skin-deep. As we have said, each tiny cell that makes up our body contains parts called sex chromosomes. These sex chromosomes contain genes, which carry different information depending on whether we have been made male or female. In addition, all the cells of the body are bathed in blood containing hormones, which influence how the cells of our bodies work. Men and women have different hormones – men have testosterone and women, oestrogen and progesterone. The combination of different genetic information and different hormones means that the *whole* body works together as a man *or* a woman, and accounts for why, on average, men are taller and physically stronger than women.

Men and women generally tend to think in different ways.[3] For example, they can be different in what pleases them or makes them anxious, and how to approach a problem. Men and women are even different in what tempts them to sin. The Bible warns women about gossiping (1 Timothy 5:13),[4] while it warns men about not picking fights with each other (1 Timothy 2:8).[5] This is not to say that men don't gossip or that women never pick a fight!

The differences between men and women help a husband and wife complement each other in a marriage. Remember, to 'complement' means to act together in different ways for the good of both. The physical differences permit sexual intimacy between a husband and wife and make it possible for them to have children. They enable a woman to do things in raising a family that no man can do – to become pregnant, to give birth to a child and to breastfeed the child in their first few months. And the natural abilities of the husband and wife complement each other as well. A husband exercises his skills as leader and provider for his wife and children, while a wife is generally attracted to the responsibility of caring for and nurturing the family.

If we forget how deep and significant these differences are, it makes us vulnerable to thinking wrongly that our sex / gender is just an 'overcoat' which we can change whenever we want.

Unhappy with their sex

Being male or female is described as the 'sex' of a person. Over the years, the English language has also used another word for 'sex' which is 'gender', which used to (and, as we shall see, still ought to) mean *exactly* the same thing.

However, recently some people have started using the word 'gender' to describe the sex they 'feel' inside and would like to be to the outside world. Such people have become unhappy with their God-given maleness or femaleness. They describe feeling 'trapped in the wrong body' and say that 'what people see of me is not really me'. Experiencing these feelings of unhappiness is called 'gender confusion' or 'gender dysphoria'. The word 'dysphoria' means 'a state of unease or dissatisfaction'. Though they are a man or woman, yet their desires and emotions seem to tell them that they would be happier being different. Even some children and teenagers just entering puberty are now saying and thinking such things.

Sometimes the person is so unhappy with their God-given sex that they take steps to change their physical appearance (their clothes, and possibly their body as well, through medication and / or surgery) to present themselves as the sex that they feel. This may be the opposite sex or sometimes another so-called 'gender identity' which might be a mixture of male and female, or no gender at all.

Sometimes these identities are called 'non-binary' (that is, neither male nor female). When a person tries to change their sex, it is called 'transitioning', which literally means 'changing', and may involve social, physical and legal changes. A person who is living as someone of the opposite sex to their birth sex is called a 'transgender' person.

Some children and young people say that they experience gender confusion. Usually, as they go through puberty, they will find that such feelings go away.[6] Unfortunately, despite the fact that the problem can be self-resolving, young people with gender confusion are sometimes treated with drugs which prevent them starting puberty (puberty blockers), then with hormones of the opposite sex, and after the age of 18, offered surgery which attempts to make their body look like someone of the opposite sex. There is good evidence that puberty blockers make gender confusion worse and their use makes it more likely that the person will try to change their sex permanently.[7] Because puberty blockers stop a developing young person going into puberty at the normal time, they affect the person's growth and maturity, and damage bone development.[8] Tragically, taking opposite sex hormones may also permanently affect a person's fertility.[9]

Is transitioning the answer?

God has designed us to work rightly and happily when our minds and bodies work in a co-ordinated or integrated way. The problem in gender dysphoria is that the mind thinks and desires things in the wrong way, causing sadness and dissatisfaction. The obvious way of resolving this would be to help the mind think and desire in the right way, sometimes through counselling. Instead of this, people are often encouraged to resolve the problem by bringing their body into line with their wrong thinking.

If they go along the pathway of trying to change their sex, they are trying to do the impossible. They also risk damaging a healthy body while continuing to experience mental distress. Though some people who transition say that they feel relieved, many remain very unhappy with their situation. Some have realised that they are actually worse off, with both a damaged body and a disturbed mind, and have tried to go back to their original sex. This is called 'detransitioning'. This is possible, but some of the body changes do not reverse easily, if at all. For example, some women are left with a permanently changed voice from the past use of male sex hormones.[10]

How do the desires of gender dysphoria measure up against God's standards?

Let us think about it in light of the principles which God has given us in the Ten Commandments.

Being discontent

God wants us to be content with everything that he has given us. God has made us male or female (Genesis 1:27). If we desire something that we are not, this is called covetousness, which breaks God's tenth commandment, 'You shall not covet' (Exodus 20:17).

Damaging the body

Our bodies are important to God and we should care for them. Being made in God's image, our bodies are designed to glorify him. They are protected by the sixth commandment, 'Thou shalt not kill' (Exodus 20:13, AKJV), which not only preserves life, but also encourages us to protect our bodies from anything that would damage them. The process of transitioning weakens or disfigures the body through using cross-sex hormones or surgery.

Living a lie

God is the God of truth. He wants us to live by the truth. The person who wants to change their sex is not living in the truth. They are born male or female, but they want to be something they are not. Science tells us that taking hormones or having an operation does not fundamentally change a person's sex. A person still has sex chromosomes in every cell of their body which carry XX if you are female or XY if you are male (as shown in the diagram above). This is determined when a baby is conceived and will not change. The threat to truth does not stop with the person wanting to change sex. Transgender people often expect others to start calling them by a different name or referring to them by a different pronoun. This encourages dishonesty and thereby breaks God's ninth commandment: 'You shall not bear false witness against your neighbour' (Exodus 20:16).

Damaging marriage

One of the reasons why God has made us male and female is so that a man and woman can marry and have a family. As we have mentioned, the differences between a husband and wife allow them to work together in a complementary way and to have children.

Trying to live as a man or woman, when you are really the other, causes great confusion. For example, a man may find himself attracted towards a 'transwoman', thinking that he may make a suitable wife. He may feel deceived and heartbroken when he finds out that the person he is attracted to was born as a man. This is just one of many ways in which transgender behaviour damages marriage and so breaks the seventh commandment which, as Jesus makes clear in Matthew 5:27–28, protects marriage from all sexual immorality, including sexual confusion.[11]

In summary, we can therefore conclude that the desire to change sex tempts someone to break the Ten Commandments, which is offensive to God (Deuteronomy 22:5).[12]

Why some people have gender confusion

We are each vulnerable to different circumstances and temptations. This is not how God made us but part of the effect of living in a sinful world and having what the Bible calls a 'sinful nature'.[13] The evil one is clever. He knows where we are weak and will try to use specific circumstances to encourage us to sin.

There is not always an obvious reason why someone feels gender confusion, but for some people their life experiences or underlying mental health problems make them vulnerable to being dissatisfied with their God-given sex. Others are damaged by poor role models in the family or having been abused in some way. The harm and unhappiness someone has experienced can distort the way they see themselves. Gender confusion may occur during puberty, especially in girls who feel uncomfortable about the changes to their bodies and also the expectations on girls and women in our sexualised society.

Others may be tempted through peer pressure, or through what they see or read on social media. Recently, there has been a rapid rise in young people with these issues (see graph below showing the number of referrals to the specialist clinic for Gender Dysphoria over the period 2010–2021). There are many teenage girls who have experienced no previous problems in this area, but have suddenly decided that they want to change sex – this is sometimes called 'Rapid Onset Gender Dysphoria'.

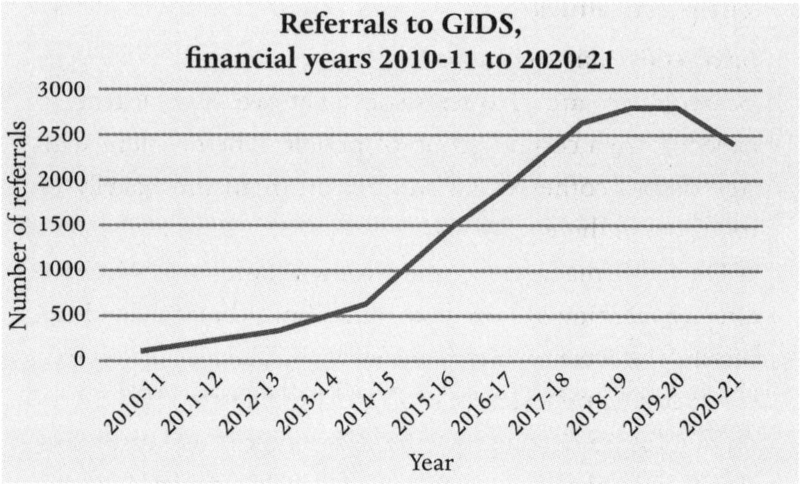

Source of information: Gender Identity Development Service (GIDS) – gids.nhs.uk/number-referrals

These young people are often heavily influenced by what they see on YouTube or Instagram and other social media platforms, where trans 'influencers' offer them an internet community which gives love and acceptance. For more information on this, see this article on social media and gender identity.[14]

The practicalities

Be careful about stereotypes

'Stereotypes' are characteristics that we have learnt to expect from a certain group of people. The problem with stereotypes comes when we rely on them too heavily or use them in the wrong way.

God has made men and women different. We have already mentioned how this affects both the body and the mind. It affects how men and women think about things – for example, preferences in friendship, hobbies and hopes for the future. Because of these differences, we can make some generalisations about how boys and girls behave. For example, *generally* girls rather than boys prefer playing with dolls or looking after a baby, and boys rather than girls *generally* prefer more aggressive sports. These could be described as stereotypes, and we must remember that not everyone fulfils a stereotype as it is only a generalisation.

Recently, some people have been using stereotypes to encourage young people to consider that they may be the wrong sex. For example, they say that if a boy likes playing with dolls or a girl likes rugby, this is a sign of a transgender tendency. Because we understand that people are not 'born in the wrong sex', we recognise that this is using stereotypes to promote a lie. We need to be careful with these things.

Meeting those with gender dysphoria

Sooner or later, you are likely to meet someone who wants

to, or has already tried to, change their sex. Young people are increasingly doing this at school age.

It is very common for someone to feel unsettled when they meet a person who wants to change their sex. You may feel distressed, especially if a friend wants to be a different sex from how you have known them, and sad because they want to go against God's good designs.

One of the reasons why this is so unsettling is that our sex is part of our identity. It is part of who we are and how we see ourselves. Many aspects of our life are bound up with our sex: what friends we have, what plans we have for life, how we dress and what we are called. So when we see someone trying to change all this, it is a big matter in a relationship. It may be unsettling, but we must ask God for help in knowing how to relate to that person. We are called by God to love those who are struggling, even if they make us feel uneasy. We must certainly avoid being unkind or antagonistic towards them. Jesus met every needy person who came to him with compassion, even though he did not endorse all their ideas.

You may be able to help someone who has gender confusion. Whatever others may be saying, it is most important to honour God and respect the person by holding to the truth that God made each of us in his image, male or female, and this cannot be changed. You can do this by listening to their anxieties and worries, by gently affirming them in their God-given sex and by encouraging them to reject any pressure that they might be feeling from unhelpful stereotyping. You can show care to a person if they feel lonely or fragile, and let them know that God is able to heal the broken-hearted (Psalm 147:3).[15] Jesus invites all who are burdened to find rest and a new identity in him (Matthew 11:28, 2 Corinthians 5:17).[16]

There is a risk that if you offer this kind of help, you may be misunderstood or even called 'transphobic'. You may lose the person's friendship and this rejection can be hard to bear. Look back at the advice we give in the chapter on homosexuality – especially under 'Helping others who experience same-sex attraction' and 'Standing firm' – because there are many similarities between helping those with same-sex attraction and those with gender dysphoria as both relate to a person's sense of identity.

There are times when your views may make you feel that you are in a minority of one, but it may not be as bad as it seems. It is easy to overestimate our isolation in a situation, as Elijah discovered when he thought that he was on his own, but God told him that there were seven thousand faithful followers (1 Kings 19:14, 18).[17] Some may secretly agree with you but not have the courage to say so. Others may admire your willingness to take a stand – and might even tell you some time later. They may also be drawn to the Lord by your faithfulness and compassion. Pray that they are.

A testimony – God works to heal gender confusion

From my earliest memories I never felt like a girl. I had an older brother and honestly thought I would grow up to be a boy like him. I used to go into primary school and tell the other kids I was really a boy undercover. That's how I felt – like a spy posing as a girl. I can't say I thought much about it consciously, but as I got older being a girl started to actually mean something to the people around me.

When I started secondary school, all the friends I seemed able to make – all the people I could relate to – were boys. I just didn't seem to get girls. They were always interested in boys and excitedly awaiting the changes their bodies were going through. For me it was all going too fast. I thought I was a boy so why was I growing up into the body of a woman? I felt so out of control. All the girls seemed like aliens to me and the boys started acting differently too.

I started frantically googling things like 'why don't I feel like a girl?' and 'why don't I understand girls if I am one?' The answer I found was that I must therefore be transgender. I came across all sorts of articles and YouTube videos about people who seemed just like me, saying that they were actually boys born into female bodies. I remember feeling so confused – I had no idea this was even possible, but if it was, then I knew that's exactly what I was going through. Further research told me that my only hope of living a happy life would involve transitioning to live as a boy, taking artificial hormones for the rest of my life, and looking forward to a slew of invasive surgeries to try and make my body resemble a man's.

At first, I didn't want to accept this. I was only twelve and I had a close relationship with Jesus, although nobody had ever told me what the Bible said about these kinds of issues. I would pray every night that God would make me wake up either feeling like a girl or looking like a boy. When nothing changed in the next five years, I decided I needed to transition to live as a man when I was 17. I started calling myself 'Ryan' and binding my chest. A year later I was injecting myself with testosterone. I felt like things were improving. I was seeing a doctor in order to get on the waiting list for these invasive surgeries. 'So long as things keep moving towards these surgeries and I have a supply of testosterone,' I thought, 'I can be happy.' I lived like that for a few years. I no longer attended church but nobody had ever told me that God might not be happy with my decision to transition.

I started university at 20 and was eagerly awaiting my first surgery. Five months later, my happiness was gone: I got my period, for the first time in three years.

The testosterone wasn't working any more and nobody could figure out why. I spent the next six months in and out of hospital, feeling suicidal. That's when God called me back to church. I started asking him what he thought of my transition. He told me to 'Consider the work of God: who can make straight what he has made crooked?' (Ecclesiastes 7:13). It took a couple of years but he brought me to the point where I understood that my gender confusion didn't come from him. He showed me where the pain had been early in my life and he worked with me to heal that pain.

In December 2019, I turned 23 and took the leap of faith to start living as a woman again for the sake of God's promises. He told me he had a plan to prosper me (Jeremiah 29:11), so the least I could do was submit to his will.[18] *It was really tough at first coming off the testosterone. I had to sacrifice everything I thought I was going to grow up to be. I also had to learn how to be okay with being a woman. But over a year later, my happiness depends on God, not on artificial hormones. God took away all the effects of the testosterone and all the gender dysphoria. It's a miracle! The biggest thing I learnt is that being a girl is not a feeling; it's the way God designed me.*

6

Men and women

God created both men and women in his image. They are, therefore, equally valuable. But he also made them different. There is a reason for this. God intends men and women to work together using their different skills and roles for the benefit of each other and the rest of society. As we've said, this is called working in a *complementary* way. Sadly, as a result of sin, men and women have often distorted the way that they should work together to bless each other. The result has been misunderstanding and hurt. This distortion has happened in two ways:

- The first way is by denying that men and women are equally valuable. It is a tragedy that in the past – and in many parts of the world even today – some men misuse their physical strength and authority to take advantage of and abuse women, rather than being considerate and respecting them. This is sometimes referred to as *male chauvinism* or, more recently, *toxic masculinity*. Sometimes the abuse is emotional; a woman is simply not given the respect and care that she deserves. We also see it in homes where there is domestic violence, and we hear of it in war zones, where women are frequently abused. It can even occur at school or college when guys objectify or belittle girls in different ways.

- The second way that men and women have distorted God's design for relationships is by rejecting the different roles for men and women. Perhaps the most common, and certainly the most popular, expression of this nowadays is promoted under the name of 'feminism', which we will now look at in more detail.

A short history of feminism

Feminism is hard to define because it has represented different views at different times. The history of feminism is often divided into different stages or 'waves'.

Early on, so-called **first wave** feminists worked towards establishing laws that gave women the right to vote, to have equal opportunities for education and employment, and to be protected from abuse in the workplace. These were God-honouring initiatives and an understandable response to the oppression of women over the years.

The **second wave** of feminism demanded equal and identical outcomes for men and women. Unless there were fifty per cent of females in every profession, it was claimed that this must be the result of discrimination. This failed to recognise that men and women often have different preferences and make different choices. Some women took their arguments further, and in the wrong direction. They increasingly saw those women who made it a priority to look after their homes and families (who society has called 'just mothers') as victims oppressed by men. Some feminists began to devalue femininity, love, marriage and motherhood, and sought to 'free' society from the God-given boundaries for sexual intimacy. Some even demanded the end of the traditional family and saw the idea of a woman having a romantic relationship with a man as male domination. Men were seen as 'oppressors' and viewed as misogynistic (women-hating) and violent. Second wave (sometimes called 'radical') feminists also demanded that women should have unrestricted sexual freedom. The sad reality, however, was that once unlimited sexual permissiveness had been unleashed, violence against women only increased.

Rage at that violence sparked off the **third wave** of feminism. Third wave feminists were determined to end sexual harassment and rape, but did not acknowledge that violence against women had been fuelled by demands for total sexual freedom. Some responded to male sexual violence by claiming the equal right to be sexually violent.

Some young feminists celebrated their own capacity to be sexual predators. Women claimed the right to dress provocatively, and the right to behave aggressively. Pornography and prostitution were promoted as 'empowering'. This only led to a greater objectification of women's bodies. It increased the sexist violence which the third wave was so furious about.

In turn, there was even greater hatred of men as an 'oppressor class'. Third wave feminism fed into 'identity politics' (where society is divided between 'oppressors' and the 'oppressed'). Men were put in the 'oppressor' class. Women were viewed as 'victims'. The 'war between the sexes' only deepened.

The tragedy of identity politics is that it sets people against each other. God's intention is for us to love our neighbour and seek the common good. It is simply not true that all males are evil predators.

By around 2010, there had been a huge rise in access to violent pornography. This in turn increased the tendency to view women as objects and led to an increase in violent behaviour and sexual harassment. The #MeToo movement was a collective shout out against abuse, and this fed into the **fourth wave** of feminism.

A young woman called Soma Sara shared her experience of 'rape culture' on Instagram in the summer of 2020. This led to the establishment of the 'Everyone's Invited' website, which has received many thousands of testimonies of girls who have experienced sexual violence at school, college or in social situations. Many had allowed someone to take explicit images of them, but then found that these were shared widely over various messaging platforms.

All abuse is an appalling outworking of sin. The instinct that justice should be done is God-given. But the response to abuse must be to avoid further sin and abuse by promoting God's designs. So let's go back to the beginning of creation and see how God designed men and women so that they were able to work together.

God's design – how it was originally

In the beginning God created Adam in his image and gave him the task of looking after and cultivating the earth. God then declared 'It is not good that the man should be alone' (Genesis 2:18), so he created Eve, also made in God's image, to be Adam's helper.

God placed Adam as head over his wife, just as God was over him, yet this in no way undermined the equal value of Adam and Eve who were both made in God's image. Eve was exactly the helper and companion that Adam needed. Adam was clearly thrilled to meet her and take her as his wife (Genesis 2:23).[1] They were designed to work in a complementary way to care for the garden which God had given Adam – 'to work it and keep it' (Genesis 2:15). Adam and Eve were created differently, and God would be glorified as they carried out their different roles and responsibilities as leader and helper.

How sin damaged the original design

Adam and Eve sinned by disobeying God in eating from the tree of the knowledge of good and evil. Though Eve was the first to eat the forbidden fruit, Adam failed to protect Eve from Satan's tempting scheme and then joined Eve in her sin by also eating the fruit. We see from the fact that God questioned Adam in Genesis 3:9–11, that God held Adam supremely responsible for the tragic events of the Fall because of his role as head.[2]

Sadly, when Adam and Eve fell into sin, everything was spoiled. This included the God-given balance between man and woman. The loving and fruitful relationship of leader and helper between Adam and Eve would be damaged then and in all future generations. When God's design is rejected, God is dishonoured and hurt results.

How God's good designs are being damaged today

Feminism, as it has unfolded, rejects God's good design. Feminists have sometimes asked some good questions. They were right to be outraged by oppression and exploitation, but the strategies they turned to only increased the scale of oppression and exploitation. Women and children have not been liberated by rejection of God's boundary markers, including his good plan for marriage and family. Instead, women have been betrayed by many feminist ideals.[3]

Feminists define being 'equal' as being 'identical', expressed in having exactly the same roles and responsibilities for men and women. Such a perspective sees a person's value, and therefore the route to equality, as determined by what they do. It is easy to fall into this way of thinking. This opposes the biblical understanding of men and women having distinctive roles which are of *equal* value but *different* and *complementary*. We need to recognise that each person's value is based on being made in God's image and, for the Christian believer, who they have become through faith in Jesus Christ (Ephesians 1:3–6).[4]

However, this is not the whole story. Feminism is not just an attack on complementarity and distinctions between the sexes. At its heart, it rejects all male authority, especially when expressed in the 'patriarchal family' – God's design of the family headed up by the husband (see 1 Corinthians 11:3).[5] In attacking the patriarchal family so much is rejected and destroyed: marriage, family life, sexual purity, romance and the privilege of raising children.

Christians are called to be watchful. Sadly today, even in Christian homes, the practical effects of feminism are being felt. Some men lack the confidence to head up their family effectively, feeling threatened by the perception that their authority is unjustified. Some men may even forsake their role altogether, leaving fatherless families. Women are encouraged that they can 'have it all' – a fulfilling career while also overseeing a home and raising children. It can be stressful and exhausting for women to juggle their lives to maintain both roles and this may lead to a husband and wife living parallel lives. As a result, many important things such as family meals, time spent together as a family discussing important issues, learning from the Bible or simply playing games and having fun can easily get squeezed out.

A feminist worldview has become an accepted view in our society. You will hear radical feminist ideals promoted in the media and by the government. However, it is not only the secular world that has promoted distortions. Some Christian churches reject the biblical distinction between the sexes, either because they do not believe in the authority of the Bible, or because they believe that it has to be modernised for today's world. They do not accept that such principles are set down in the Bible by an unchanging and all-wise God. This attitude has led to the appointment of women as church leaders (so rejecting the principles of 1 Timothy 3). It is easy to be taken in by these false ideas, especially if they come from within the church.

The rejection of God's good design also affects how men act. God has granted men strength and authority for a good purpose – to help and protect those whom God has given them responsibility for. The Bible describes a beautiful interdependence of husband and wife (see Ephesians 5:22–33). When men misuse their strength and authority, or do not accept their responsibilities, they damage those around them. Within marriage, instead of working together as a team, the relationship of trust between husband and wife falls apart. The wife, rather than feeling secure and affirmed, becomes fearful and defensive, and may be tempted to seize control. Children, rather than being disciplined by a firm but patient father, are often subjected to anger and aggression.

God redeems the situation by showing us how to live

As we have seen, both feminism (certainly in its recent forms) and toxic masculinity are forms of rebellion against God's good design and have caused much damage. But we serve a God who is kind and gracious and does not treat us, either individually or as a society, as our sins deserve (Psalm 103:10).[6] Instead, God teaches his people how they should live according to his wisdom.

It was as Christianity spread through parts of the world that the dignity of womanhood was lifted up. It was in the time of the Christian Roman Emperor Constantine that women began to have the right to own property and the right to be guardians of their children. Previously only men had had these rights. Christians were also important in pioneering the opening up of education to girls (as well as boys), both at home and abroad.[7] Far from repressing women, true Christianity has demanded that women are treated with the same respect that Christ himself showed women when he lived on this earth. When Christianity is strong in a community, this positively impacts the lives of women.

Essential differences

The Bible is clear that our femininity or masculinity is an essential part of who we are. This is evident from the first description of the creation of mankind in Genesis 1:27:

So God created man in his own image,
in the image of God he created him;
male and female he created them.

You must not be confused into thinking that your femininity or masculinity is like a cloak that covers you, as current gender ideology might suggest. Rather it reaches to the very core of who we are, as a defining quality. This is reflected in biological distinctions between the sexes. As we've said, every cell of our body has either an XY (in men) or XX (in women) pair of sex chromosomes, our tissues are constantly bathed by different hormones, and our male or female anatomy is obviously quite distinct.

We serve a God who has created us to enjoy the distinctions in roles and responsibilities between men and women – and this is reflected in many verses, especially in the New Testament. Such distinctions are not simply our society's convention or culture – but written into our creation and shown to us by the word of God!

We learn from the Bible that our situation in life is a gift from God to be used to serve him in the best way possible. This may include serving God as a single person or being married (1 Corinthians 7:7).[8] At the time of reading this, it is very unlikely that you know whether or not you will marry later in life and you will probably feel differently about this at different times. But God has a plan for your life. As young men and women, it is important to prepare yourselves in the best way for whatever he has planned for you in the future. What follows is a summary of how you, as young men and women, can do this in practical ways.

Young men

You need to think about your future role of providing for yourself and for others. The Bible encourages us to work hard, remembering that we are ultimately working for God: 'Whatever you do, work heartily, as for the Lord and not for men' (Colossians 3:23). Work hard at your studies and be ambitious to excel in what you do, not for your own glory or to feed your pride but to glorify God by making the most of your knowledge, skills and opportunities to serve others through whatever job God calls you to do.

You also need to grow your leadership skills, especially with the possibility of wanting to protect and support a wife and children in the future. The qualities of leadership are usually learned by submitting to other authority figures at home, at school, at work or in the church. If you do not have a father to follow, look for other godly role models in your church. They will stand out to you as men who lead not by domineering or dictating to others, but by encouraging and building others up, and prayerfully putting Christ at the centre of their lives. Christian young men can also learn through taking on humble roles of service in the church or sharing in the running of a Christian group at college, university or at work.

Leadership can be tough, as well as being a great privilege. It may involve stepping up and taking initiative as well as taking responsibility if or when things go wrong. This may involve taking self-denying risks for the sake of others and for God, for example, to your reputation or future job prospects. Men even need to be willing to risk their lives, as many have done in the past to give us the freedoms in our society that we currently enjoy.

In the Old Testament, Boaz showed good qualities of male leadership, protection and provision for his future bride, Ruth (Ruth chapters 2–4). Notice how Boaz cares for and protects his workers (2:4), takes initiative to care for, protect and provide for Ruth and is grateful and thoughtful towards her (2:8–16), acts with respect and sexual purity in tempting circumstances (3:8–14) and takes initiative in clarifying matters with the 'close relative' (4:1–11).

The Lord Jesus was the perfect model of self-denying male leadership. He modelled to his disciples the loving and humble behaviour he expected from them by washing their feet (John 13:1–17), and was the perfect model of submission to his Father's will when he faced death on the cross in order to bring salvation to those who trust in him (Matthew 26:36–42). We also see self-denying leadership in the life of the Apostle Paul who faced the prospect of 'imprisonment and afflictions', and said, 'But I do not account my life of any value nor as precious to myself, if only I may finish my course and the ministry that I received from the Lord Jesus' (Acts 20:23–24).

You can also learn from the example of past godly men. It is encouraging to read of famous missionaries such as David Brainerd and Henry Martyn, who gave up their lives in order to take the gospel to others.[9] There have also been many business entrepreneurs such as William Colgate and Henry Heinz who were inspired by their Christian faith.[10]

Both in the Bible and in history, men have used their leadership and strength to protect those who are vulnerable, especially women and children. One expression of this protective role is to treat young women with respect. The Apostle Paul encouraged Timothy to relate to 'younger women as sisters, in all purity' (1 Timothy 5:2). It is not right for a young man to take advantage of the vulnerability of a woman; rather he should seek to protect her by controlling his sexual desires. A respectful and protective attitude towards women used to be called chivalry, and men need to rediscover this virtue.

This attitude applies when there are no girls or women around, just as much as when you are with them. For example, how do you talk about them with your male friends? If someone makes a degrading or suggestive remark about a girl you know, it can be tempting to join the crowd. Instead, speak up to show respect and protect your female friend and explain why you do not want to talk about her in that way. Similarly, avoid any material that promotes wrong sexual thoughts about women or demeans them (see chapter 3, *Pornography*).

If you are going out with a girl, you have a special responsibility to behave protectively towards her (and to yourself) by making sure you both avoid situations that might lead to sexual thoughts or behaviour. This will demonstrate genuine love and care for your girlfriend, and should lead you to initiate a discussion on the setting of boundaries for your relationship.

Young women

Eve was created to be Adam's helper. Many parents have observed that helpfulness is hard-wired into their daughters, even at an early age. The characteristic of helpfulness is not limited to marriage and family life. There will be no shortage of opportunities to put helpfulness into practice in society and especially among your church family. As you progress through school, you will notice God-given talents and abilities that you may want to develop for your future. We do not always know how God might use these gifts, but it is right to want to develop them and to see him use them for his glory.

Some women are called to marry and have children. Though such a calling may not be held in high esteem by our society, homemaking and motherhood are highly honoured in God's sight (Titus 2:4–5) and full of his blessing (1 Timothy 2:15).[11] Whatever happens in the future, it is good to learn skills to use at home, such as cooking and other aspects of creativity that you enjoy, in addition to pursuing your academic interests.

Our current society puts huge emphasis on how a woman looks. This can cause girls a lot of anxiety and stress, but also divert attention from the qualities that really matter. When Abraham's servant was sent to find a wife for Abraham's son Isaac (see Genesis 24), his first concern was not her looks. He asked God to show him a woman who would not only give him a drink after his long journey in the dusty desert, but offer to water his ten camels as well (this probably meant drawing about 1,000 litres of water!) Happily, Rebekah did just that (verses 19–20). She showed that she was kind, generous and hardworking, as well as being attractive in appearance (verse 16).

In Proverbs 31:10–31, we meet another excellent wife. The central focus of her life is her household whose material needs (verses 15, 21) and spiritual needs (verse 26) are her constant concern. There is no hint of this wife being passive in her life of service. Her work includes buying land for a vineyard and making tapestries. Through this she supports her husband in his leadership role (verse 23), blesses her children (verse 28) and cares for the practical needs of the poor (verse 20). She does all this because she fears the Lord (verse 30).

There are many outstanding examples of women who have been used by God both inside and outside the home. Sarah Edwards, the wife of 18th century New England minister Jonathan Edwards, was the anchor in their family home. Sarah supported the family through the ups and downs of Jonathan's ministry, as well as bereavement and poverty after his ejection as minister in Northampton. Josephine Butler, with the support of her husband, and after the death of a young daughter, devoted her life to promoting higher education for women and to protecting the wellbeing of vulnerable women in Victorian England and abroad.

Godly femininity avoids being aggressive and tries to show 'a gentle and quiet spirit, which in God's sight is very precious' (1 Peter 3:4). It also avoids provoking the opposite sex. It can be easy to provoke or manipulate young men who may be struggling with sexual temptation and the difficulties of singleness, as you may be yourself. Try to avoid any kind of sexual impurity in what you think, what you say and how you act.

Be thoughtful and dress modestly (1 Timothy 2:9–10).[12] You can still fulfil a God-given desire to look feminine and attractive without making your appearance an idol. You will most likely have heard the feminist claim that women have the right to wear whatever they like without any consideration as to how this affects men. However, this is not what the Bible teaches. We are commanded many times in the Bible to 'love one another' (John 13:34, Romans 12:10).[13] This means that both sexes have a responsibility to think of others rather than themselves and show consideration to others in the way they dress and behave. However, it is important to understand that you are not responsible for the sexually immoral behaviour of others: if you become the victim of a crime such as sexual harassment or assault, the actions of the perpetrator should be reported to the appropriate authorities.

If you are dating a boy, you might have a closer relationship with him than other male friends – for example, in talking of things that you would not share with others. However, you are not married, so avoid sexual intimacy or anything that tempts you in this direction, such as spending long times together alone, and especially indoors. You both have an equal responsibility to behave in a God-honouring way, so establish your boundaries together.

Roles for men and women in marriage

In the Bible, the practical outworking of how men and women relate to each other is most fully addressed in the context of marriage (especially in Ephesians 5) and in how the church should function (for example, 1 Timothy 2 and 3, but this is outside the remit of this book).

In the New Testament, the husband is described as the head of his wife (Ephesians 5:23), who is, therefore, required to submit to him (5:22). The word 'submit' has been distorted by society. It has been used by men as an excuse to treat women as inferior and make them compliant. This led to the word being considered as completely negative and many people rejecting the idea of submission completely.

In contrast, submission described in the Bible is very different. The Bible speaks of God's people 'submitting to one another out of reverence for Christ' (Ephesians 5:21). In helping us understand how this is to work specifically in marriage, the Bible explains that marriage is a picture of the relationship between Christ and his church. It involves the wife respecting her husband and supporting him in his leadership role as the church submits to Christ. Her husband is required to love her in a self-sacrificial way which is compared to the sacrifice Jesus Christ made for his people when he died on the cross (verse 25). This responsibility is God's way of ensuring that women and children are cared for and protected, and the family is a secure environment where decisions can be made and disagreements dealt with in a loving and respectful way.

You may be wondering whether any of this is relevant to you. The prospect of marriage and family may seem far away. Yet, just as you will choose which subjects to study with a view to a future job, it is also important to think about your relationships now with a view to possible marriage and family life in the future. When men and women try to work together in the ways that God has designed, although they will not get it right all the time, it will be a blessing to them and to all who are impacted by their lives.

James and Catherine's testimony

Here is the testimony of one Christian couple:

We have been married for 20 years. Looking back, we can see how God has brought us together as a team for his purpose and glory. We have much in common, both in our background and now also in our interests. We have both experienced growing up in loving Christian homes, have two siblings, have become doctors, love the outdoors and are very social people. We are also very aware of our differences and love the uniqueness of the different personalities and gifts God has given us. We also believe in the complementary roles for marriage that the Bible teaches about and think these differences have made us stronger as a unit.

We are aware that in today's society it is not culturally acceptable to acknowledge any difference between men and women. However, for us, these differences are not something we have ever felt threatened by. We believe as Christians that Jesus must be the Lord of our marriage and that means each of us playing our God-given part.

Catherine says: As a wife, the word submission used in the Bible does not mean I am of less value or less able than my husband, nor does it mean I must blindly follow every suggestion made by him. Our decisions over the years have been joint and debated as equals with respect for each other's hopes and fear. Ultimately, however, I believe the Bible encourages me to allow my husband to lead our family. For me personally, this meant I wanted to allow my husband to take the lead in his career. During my medical training, I particularly enjoyed specialities that focused on children and care of the elderly, both of which were hospital-based careers. As a married woman,

I instead decided to become a GP as I realised that this offered more flexibility and having two doctors with hospital jobs would be likely to make family life difficult. We ended up adopting two boys in 2011 and a girl in 2016, since which time I have been able to work as a GP one day a week. This has allowed time to look after the needs of our family which has included being available to homeschool one of my children for 18 months when he needed special help with his education.

James says: As a husband, I am aware that my most important duty before God is to love my wife. This means being other-person centred and putting myself out for her sake. It also means having to be prepared to forgo things I want at times. Parenting our three children who have been in the looked-after system brings particular challenges and perhaps even more need for a father to be present and available. This has meant I have needed to decline various positions of responsibility at my work and not attend certain conferences when I would be away overnight, in order to support my wife in managing our children's needs.

Our faith in Christ has been crucial in accepting our differences as a married couple and parents of our children. We believe that with our identity as God's children, we can have security in who God made us to be and that he will use those differences to bless us and others around us.

7

Abortion

God's good design

Most parents greet the news that they are expecting a baby with great joy and excitement. Have you ever asked your parents how they felt when they realised that you were on the way? Do they remember their thrill at the positive pregnancy test, or their wonder at seeing you bouncing around in the womb during an ultrasound scan? These are exciting moments for parents.

The Bible describes children as a 'heritage from the Lord' (Psalm 127:3). A heritage is a precious gift which has been given to the parents by God to be a blessing. This gift is no ordinary object. Rather, most parents recognise very early on in the pregnancy that it is the gift of a *new life*; they refer to him or her as 'their baby' and many feel a strong sense of love towards their child in the womb.

There are many references in the Bible to the unborn child which testify that he or she is a human life, made in

God's image. Only a living person can leap for joy – John the Baptist did this in the womb at the recognition of Jesus, who was in Mary's womb.[1] The life of the unborn child begins at conception, the moment when a woman's egg is fertilised by a male sperm. Jesus took on human form from the moment that he was conceived in Mary's womb through the power of the Holy Spirit. Psalm 51:5 also testifies to life beginning at conception with the words 'in sin did my mother conceive me'.[2] Here David is describing his earliest days in the womb. From his conception, David must have been alive in order to have a sinful nature.

In Psalm 139:13–16, King David also records how God forms the unborn child in the womb as the work of a master craftsman with great skill:

For you formed my inward parts;
you knitted me together in my mother's womb.
I praise you, for I am fearfully and wonderfully made.
Wonderful are your works;
my soul knows it very well.
My frame was not hidden from you,
when I was being made in secret,
intricately woven in the depths of the earth.
Your eyes saw my unformed substance;
in your book were written, every one of them,
the days that were formed for me,
when as yet there was none of them.

With life there are responsibilities

Life is precious. Because the unborn child has the infinite value of life made in God's image, there comes a responsibility to protect and provide for him or her. Many pregnant mothers express this responsibility by doing all they can to help their baby grow well – they eat well, avoid things that might damage the baby such as alcohol and smoking, and keep healthy by doing some regular exercise. God has given us a command to do everything to protect the life of another person.[3]

The facts about abortion

Abortion is the termination or ending of a pregnancy before birth. Although an abortion can occur spontaneously (often called a miscarriage) for reasons such as illness in the mother or the unborn, when we refer to abortion here, we mean the *deliberate* ending of the life of an unborn baby.

Abortion was common in Greek and Roman society, when it not only destroyed the life of the baby but was also very dangerous for the mother. As Christianity spread in the early history of the church, the practice of abortion was challenged, and the lives of many unborn babies and their mothers were saved.[4]

Abortion has been permitted in law in the UK since 1967 and in the US since 1973. Both in the UK and the US, the number of abortions has risen steadily since its legalisation. In 1969 (the first full year) there were over 54,000 abortions in England and Wales; now over 200,000 are performed each year (see the chart below). That is equivalent to about 560 abortions each day.[5] In the US, abortion rates peaked in 1980 and have been in decline since but still run at over 600,000 each year or over 1,643 per day.[6] Since its legalisation, over 9.5 million abortions have been performed in the UK.[7] In the US, the figure is over 42 million.[8]

In the UK, about one in four pregnancies end in abortion, and in the US, it has been about one in five.[9]

Total abortions per year in England and Wales

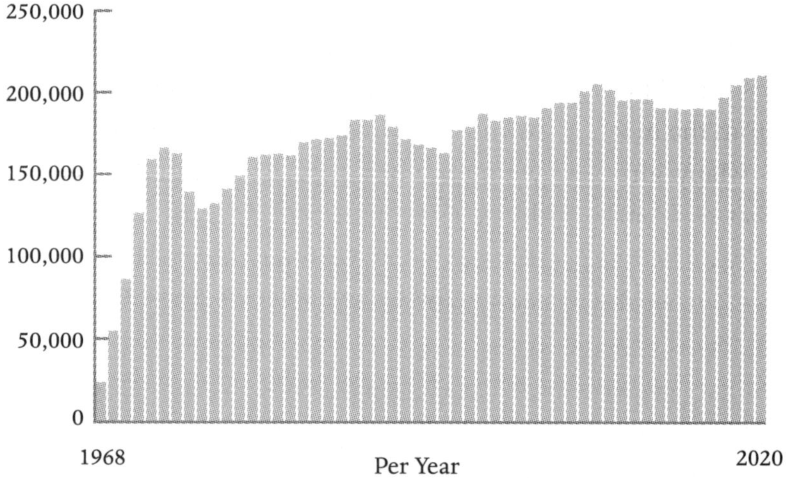

Source of information: https://www.gov.uk/government/statistics/abortion-statistics-for-england-and-wales-2020

In the UK, most abortions are funded by the National Health Service and carried out in local hospitals, or private clinics, but still paid for by the NHS. In the US, most abortions are carried out by private or not-for-profit abortion providers (often funded by state taxes). In the UK, the law allows a woman to have an abortion up to 24 weeks – just over halfway through the pregnancy (or, in the case of a baby with an abnormality, abortion is allowed any time up to birth).[10] In the US, the law varies between states.

An abortion can be performed early in a pregnancy by the mother taking two medicines, one that kills her unborn child and the second that makes her womb expel the baby (known as a medical abortion). The alternative is to perform a surgical procedure in which the unborn child is removed from the mother's womb (known as a surgical abortion).

Many girls and young women have been misinformed that the unborn baby is 'just a bunch of cells' or a 'bit of jelly'. The truth is very different. The heart starts beating by four weeks' gestation, and by eight weeks' gestation he or she is recognisable as a tiny baby.[11] Two weeks later, at a time when many abortions are carried out, the baby has limbs and internal organs, although the baby is only about 5 cm long. This rapid early development again reminds us that we are 'fearfully and wonderfully made' (Psalm 139:14).

Both medical and surgical abortions can sometimes be complicated by pain, infection and bleeding in the mother. There is increasing concern in the scientific community that the unborn baby feels pain, and therefore abortions will cause pain to the unborn baby, especially when performed later in pregnancy.[12]

Why does a woman choose to have an abortion?

We have observed how many parents delight in discovering that they are expecting and, from a very early stage of pregnancy, feel a love and sense of responsibility towards their unborn child. But tragically some respond very differently to the news of becoming parents. Instead of delight at their new role and responsibility, they are upset at finding themselves pregnant. Such a pregnancy is sometimes called a 'crisis pregnancy', which is often an unplanned pregnancy. What is the cause of this crisis? They might feel that they are not in the right circumstances to raise this child. The woman or her partner, especially if they are still young, may feel concerned about the impact childbearing would have on their life plans.

Easily the most common underlying reason for a crisis pregnancy is that the woman has become pregnant outside of marriage. If people kept sex for marriage, the thought of having an abortion would be so much less common. A single woman cannot always depend on the support of her partner. Some men, finding they have caused a woman to become pregnant, refuse to take responsibility for a child and encourage the woman to seek an abortion. Without the support of the child's father, a woman who becomes pregnant may feel vulnerable and anxious. She may feel that everything she has planned and hoped for has come crashing down around her, and she is likely to deeply regret the sexual involvement that led to the pregnancy.

Sadly, though less commonly, abortion can also be sought within marriage. This could be because of unfaithfulness within the marriage, or because the couple feel unable to cope with another child.

Others face extremely difficult circumstances that go beyond the big challenges of being a single mother or having an unplanned baby in the family. They may discover that their child has an abnormality and will need special care for many months or years to come. Still other women find themselves pregnant after the horrific ordeal of being forced into sexual intimacy (called rape).

It is often assumed these days that abortion is the best way to deal with such difficult circumstances and that 'getting rid of the problem' is the solution. Often the woman will be quickly referred to an abortion clinic, and sometimes feel pressurised to go through with the abortion by her boyfriend or family. Regrettably, there is often very little opportunity to think carefully about what she is considering. Despite the pressure to have an abortion, some women in these circumstances choose to keep their baby and, having made the decision, find the strength to bring up the child with the help and support of friends and family. Many look back and are glad that they made that decision.

Another option for a woman or couple facing a crisis pregnancy is to give the child to loving adoptive parents. There are increasing numbers of married couples who would love to adopt a baby and give that child a happy and secure home to grow up in. Adoption is a very special subject for Christians to consider. Adoption is God's idea – God adopts those who repent and believe in the Lord Jesus into his family.[13]

Pro-life or pro-choice?

When thinking about the subject of abortion, you may have heard the terms 'pro-life' and 'pro-choice' and wondered what they actually mean. These words represent totally opposite views about unborn life and abortion.

Those who believe that nothing should be done to actively destroy the life of the unborn are described as 'pro-life'. Many of those who hold this pro-life belief are people who understand that it is God who gives life and that life should not be destroyed by abortion or by the use of any contraception that can destroy the already fertilised egg.

In contrast, people who hold a 'pro-choice' view believe in the autonomy (which literally means 'self-rule') of the mother. They believe that a woman has the right to decide what happens to her own body and this includes the unborn baby in her womb. They assume that she has freedom to make her own moral choices even if this conflicts with God's laws. This attitude also assumes wrongly that the unborn baby has no rights.

Thinking biblically about abortion

However difficult the circumstances might be, having an

abortion goes against God's laws that are outlined in the Bible. The sixth commandment, 'You shall not murder' (Exodus 20:13), forbids the deliberate ending of human life. The unborn child is especially vulnerable because he or she is small and immature and cannot defend himself or herself nor cry out for help. God tells us in the Bible to take care of the poor and needy, especially those who cannot defend themselves.[14] This responsibility begins right from the moment of conception when a new unique human being is created bearing the image of God. As the creator of human life, God could be described as wholeheartedly 'pro-life'. Because of the clarity of God's word in the Bible, we can be sure that God hates abortion. For this reason, however difficult the circumstances and however she may feel, having an abortion will never bring long-term peace and blessing to the mother, her partner and family, nor to a country which permits it so freely.

After an abortion

You might think that most women would be very relieved once they have had their abortion. The responsibilities of motherhood are over, and life might return to normal. Though initially this might be the case, in the longer term it is often not so. Tragically, there are books filled with unhappy testimonies of women after abortion.[15] Even from very soon after the abortion, many women (and sometimes men) are filled with regret, sadness or guilt at the loss of life. A woman may suffer considerable emotional pain for years to come. If she later has a child, she may think as much about the child she chose to abort as the one she has chosen to keep.

It is often very hard for a woman to talk about what she is suffering, especially if she recognises that she is partly responsible for what has happened. It can be hard for her to know whom to share her feelings with. Very often her boyfriend has deserted her, and her friends and family may not want to talk about it, especially if they have encouraged her to go ahead with the abortion.

It is encouraging to remember that God offers complete forgiveness to those who repent of what they have done wrong (Psalm 103:10–12).[16] Many women have been helped by taking part in counselling or a recovery course.[17]

Is there any hope?

This testimony from Mary Lou is in some ways an encouraging account because, through the pain and sadness, God brought her to himself and forgave her for having ended the life of her child.[18]

> *I had an abortion at 17 because I was frightened, and I allowed my fear to control me. I was frightened of the consequences of living at home, and being single, and people getting to know I was sexually active. I regret that I made a mistake to cover up a wrong choice. I regret my abortion.*

At the time no one counselled me; no one explained what was going to happen. No one said I had a choice. No one explained to me that living inside me was a growing and perfectly formed 14-week-old baby girl. I was to find all these things out later.

Years later I found myself on a hospital ward awaiting fertility tests. The nurse came in and drew the curtain around my bed, as they were talking about the termination of pregnancy to another lady across the ward from me. Instantly, this dark cloud descended upon me, as the full weight of what I had done years before began to surround me.

I desperately wanted a child and I was having difficulty. All around me women were aborting their babies, and I couldn't have one. They were getting rid of them, and I couldn't have one. I had aborted my only chance of giving birth to my own child. As a young person I had had so many dreams. After my abortion I thought that I was never going to be good at anything because I had made such a dreadful mistake. I was afraid and I felt that way for years, living under that cloud of fear. I felt that I had committed the worst crime ever and I was always afraid of being found out. I buried these emotions, tried to cover them up and get on as best I could. But I felt that deep down I was useless.

But in order to live a healthy life, you cannot live in denial. It does break; you have to come out from under it. The protective wall begins to crumble. Mine began to crumble when I laid eyes on the baby boy that I had waited so many years to adopt. The pain I felt for the daughter I had lost was overwhelming. But I didn't know then how to express my grief because women who have had an abortion are not allowed to express their grief or feel sad for the decision they have made.

I went through months on a roller-coaster of emotions. So excited – elated at being a mum finally for the first time – and realising the grief that I held in my heart for the child that I had aborted. I could no longer deny or keep it buried. I did find a sympathetic counsellor who helped me through these emotions and helped me to come face to face with each area of my life that the abortion had affected.

I did eventually find peace and forgiveness from God and from my parents. God helped me to discover his love, his grace and most of all his mercy. I discovered that he was there the whole time. He was allowing me to make my mistakes. They were my choices. I didn't want to make his choices. He allowed me to make my own choices. He watched as I made one mistake after another. He wept with me as I wept over the loss of my child. He was waiting with open arms as I eventually opened my heart to him completely and allowed him to come in and heal me of this hurt.

Sexual purity and marriage

8

Personal purity

The book of Proverbs (especially the first nine chapters) contains important instruction from a faithful father to his son. It is striking how many verses are taken up warning him against sexual temptation (e.g. Proverbs 2:16–19, 5:3–8). This is because the father knows just how important this is for his son (and much applies to a daughter as well). His instructions become all the more relevant as you grow up, and later move away from home, when you will be less accountable to your parents and those in your current church family who know you well.

Temptation

Temptation is a pull to think, say or do something wrong. Temptation to sexual sin comes both from inside us (sometimes known as 'the flesh') and from the outside (sometimes known as 'the world'). Both the flesh and the world, usually working together, can be used by Satan to tempt you to do wrong.

Temptation can come from inside you. During or after puberty, as your hormones kick in, you will probably feel an attraction to the opposite sex. God designed you this way. Sexual attraction can lead to sexual desires. We want what we are attracted to! If we let them, sexual desires can become very powerful and can feel like they need to be fulfilled immediately. However, not all sexual desires should be fulfilled, and certainly not straightaway. It is God's will that we control sexual desires until we find ourselves in the right context to fulfil them, which is in marriage.

Temptations also come from outside of you and can stir up sexual desires. We now live in a very sexualised society with all kinds of wrong expectations and practices – this book focuses on six issues which result from rejecting God's ways. Of these, pornography is probably the most immediate threat to your sexual purity, especially if you are a young man. The immoral woman described in Proverbs 7, who is 'lurking at every corner' (verse 12 NKJV), is now lurking in every mobile phone.

Be careful what you think about, what websites you browse, who you follow on social media, what books you read, what films you watch, what music you listen to and what friends you hang out with. It is easy to find yourself being squeezed into a wrong way of thinking without being aware of it. Christians are encouraged to 'Look carefully then how you walk, not as unwise but as wise' (Ephesians 5:15).

Sadly, fewer and fewer films, books or websites, unless prepared by faithful Christians, are sympathetic to a biblical perspective on *any* of the topics addressed in this book. Rather, they are likely to promote exactly the opposite, perhaps hidden in humour, documentaries and soap opera drama. Even if you think you are watching or reading with your 'spiritual antennae' on, you can be subtly drawn into the world's way of thinking.

Here are some questions to ask yourself about what you read and who you follow:

- Do they over-romanticise relationships so that they are unreal?
- Do they make you discontent?
- Are they visually or emotionally provocative?
- Do they trivialise, affirm, or glamorise sin?

Let us look at how God offers to help us avoid temptation and relate to the opposite sex in a way that honours him.

Living as a Christian

It is difficult to resist sexual temptation without God's help. The father's chief instruction to his son in the book of Proverbs is to fear the Lord (Proverbs 3:7).[1] This means to respect God by trusting his ways are best for us in every aspect of life. Only then will his son 'keep to the paths of the righteous' (2:20).

In order to receive this help, you must be in a relationship with God by becoming a Christian. This involves repenting and believing in the Lord Jesus as your Saviour. Repentance means being sorry for your sin and coming to a merciful God to be forgiven. It involves turning away from your sin with God's help. True repentance also involves a hatred and sadness over past sins and a determination not to repeat them.

Some Christians can feel particularly guilty about sexual sin. The good news is that, however serious the sin, the Lord Jesus took upon himself the punishment we deserve when he died on the cross. If someone turns to God in faith and asks him for forgiveness, God promises to forgive them their sins (1 John 1:9).[2] No guilt or condemnation remains (Romans 8:1),[3] but rather a new start with a clean slate. This is God's gift to all who believe.

After conversion, a Christian wants to show his or her love for God by trusting that his ways are best, and then following them. The Lord Jesus reminds us that if we love him, we will keep his commandments (John 14:23).[4] God gives every Christian the help of the Holy Spirit. Among other things, the Holy Spirit can give us the strength that we need to be self-controlled and patient (Galatians 5:22–23).[5] Unlike conversion, which is instant, the Holy Spirit progressively changes our hearts so that we want to please God more and more in our lives.

It is essential that you keep speaking with God in prayer as you face the challenges of life. The Lord's Prayer addresses our heavenly Father about our needs when we say, 'Give us this day our daily bread' (Matthew 6:11). So, when you need God's help, go to him to provide for you. The prayer also asks for protection, 'Lead us not into temptation, but deliver us from evil' (Matthew 6:13). Prayer is an essential element in the spiritual battle as we seek to be obedient to God in our relationships (Ephesians 6:18).[6]

Know what the Bible says

The Bible is clear that sex has been designed by God as a blessing for, and only for, marriage. Many New Testament passages forbid 'sexual immorality'. For example, Paul encourages the Christians in Thessalonica to avoid sexual immorality and control ungodly desires:

> *For this is the will of God, your sanctification: that you abstain from sexual immorality; that each one of you know how to control his own body in holiness and honour.* (1 Thessalonians 4:3–4)

The word translated as 'immorality' in many modern versions means any sexual activity outside marriage, including sexual intimacy before marriage, unfaithfulness within marriage and homosexual acts.

The Bible is equally clear that our thoughts as well as our actions matter to God. We mentioned Jesus' warning about 'heart adultery' (Matthew 5:27–28) in chapter 3, *Pornography*, because it is particularly relevant to that temptation.[7] But we do not need to see wrong images to sin in our thoughts; anything that stirs us to sexual thoughts outside marriage is wrong before God. This applies throughout the whole of our lives, whether we are single or married.

You might have heard the term 'casual sex'. But before God, there is nothing casual about sex. Rather, sex is something holy, which in Hebrew, literally means 'set apart'. Sex was designed by God to be set apart for marriage. In keeping sexually pure as a single Christian, you might feel that you are missing out or that God is limiting your freedom or enjoyment. The Bible reassures us that God's commandments are for our good and given to us out of his love for us. God will bless your obedience (Deuteronomy 30:16) and protect you from harm (Psalm 119:92).[8]

Be content where you find yourself

Many of your friends may be pairing up. It may feel that you are left out or even left behind. But if you think about the dangers of sexual temptation, and the misunderstandings and false hopes that may arise, it may be wise to hold back from finding a girlfriend or boyfriend until you are ready to go out with a view to marriage. This used to be called 'courting'.

Rather than rushing to pair up, enjoy being single, recognising that this is where God wants you to be in this phase of your life. You will be able to do things that you may be unable to do later if you have the responsibilities that come with being married and having children. Put your energies into gaining the skills and qualities that you will need to serve God throughout your adult life. Above all, trust God in this important area of your life rather than trying to work things out for yourself.

Acknowledge that God's ways are best and enjoy discovering how he will keep his promise to bless you (Proverbs 3:1–10).

Take evasive action

It is most important in the matter of sexual purity to decide firmly in advance where your personal boundaries lie so that you honour God. If you wait until the moment you are faced with the decision and rely on yourself to decide in the heat of the moment, you are very likely to overstep the boundary. If you do find yourself in a situation that you do not want to be in, because you feel tempted or pressurised, you need to follow the advice of the Bible and run away (2 Timothy 2:22, 1 Corinthians 6:18).[9] Sometimes this may mean physically removing yourself from the situation. Remember how Joseph ran out of the house when Potiphar's wife tried to tempt him (Genesis 39:12).[10] In order to avoid tempting circumstances you may need to break off a relationship or block someone who sends a suggestive image to your phone.

It is not always possible to avoid temptations. Though we may feel weak and vulnerable in ourselves, it is reassuring to know that God recognises our situation and always promises to give us a way out if we ask him. Be encouraged by these words: 'No temptation has overtaken you that is not common to man. God is faithful, and he will not let you be tempted beyond your ability, but with the temptation he will also provide the way of escape, that you may be able to endure it' (1 Corinthians 10:13).

However good it may seem at the time, there are always consequences

Sexual sin may feel good at the time. The writer of Proverbs puts it like this: 'Stolen water is sweet' (Proverbs 9:17). But as the next verse warns, there are always consequences.[11]

Spiritually, there are consequences to sexual sin, because we have offended God. We will probably feel guilty and lose confidence in God's love for us (our 'assurance'). *Physically*, our bodies may suffer – sexually transmitted infections (STIs) are much more common among those who have multiple partners. STIs can be serious and cannot always be cured. And, of course, when sexual activity takes place, a child may be conceived.

Sexual sin also hurts us *emotionally*. We may feel ashamed because we know we have done something wrong. When we experience sexual intimacy we give something away to another person. When that takes place outside marriage, we may feel loss or anger because we have been used or robbed. It can also weaken our ability to bond with another person in the future. Sexual intimacy involves emotional bonding which should not be broken; this is the way God made us. We now know that this bonding happens because of the activity of hormones, such as oxytocin and vasopressin, which work in various parts of the body including the brain, where they are involved in sexual behaviour, social recognition and stress responses. This is why, for example, a person feels such pain when the person they have been intimate with does not reply to a text the next day or moves on to be with someone else.

Practically, we can damage the future by threatening marriage – our own and that of others.

Thinking about marriage

You may think that you would like to get married in the future… you may rightly recognise it as the only God-given route to having a family of your own… you can see the blessings of marriage and family life, but how does that impact your life now?

During your teenage years there are various ways that you can prepare for marriage. Studying hard for the right trade or profession may be important so that you can bring in an income. Learning to drive, to cook and to do DIY may prepare you to run a home. But however well you prepare in these ways, you can easily spoil things, including future marriage, by acting in a wrong way towards the opposite sex, especially sexually.

Some young people are rejecting marriage for the reasons explained in the next chapter. Christian young people do not need to feel like this. We can trust that marriage and sex are part of God's 'very good' design (Genesis 1:31) and full of God's blessing when experienced according to his way.[12] One way of exploring this is through going out, which gives you the opportunity to get to know someone and to decide whether you genuinely love them and want to spend the rest of your life with them in marriage. But it also brings with it some dangers.

The particular challenge of romance and going out

Many young people think that if they are in a romantic relationship, they are required to be sexually intimate. It could be that romantic feelings or the desire to feel secure in a relationship make it difficult to resist sexual temptation before marriage. Sleeping with someone does not prove your love for that person. Someone who puts pressure on you to be sexually intimate loves themselves more than they love you or God. Real love means *waiting*. By avoiding anything sexually arousing at this stage, you are honouring and protecting marriage – that of others, and also your own if that is God's plan for you in the future.

Here are some practical observations that support what God says:

- Sexual involvement stops you getting to know a person. It can distort a growing friendship and can make it difficult to know if the person you are going out with would really be a suitable wife or husband.

- Take a look at this lady's testimony online (using the QR code below).[13] Soon after getting married, she realised that she and her husband had not really got to know each other before they married and had very little in common. Their sexual intimacy had made them feel artificially close to each other.

- True romance is destroyed by sexual immorality and built up by self-control. Many girls can give testimony like this: 'I loved him, I let him, and I lost him.' Any feelings of romance turned to sadness and pain. Going out is an opportunity to learn self-control and build up trust in each other before you get married.

- If your relationship breaks up, the person you have been going out with may be someone else's future wife or husband, as you may be too. Many married couples look back wishing that they had had fewer boyfriends or girlfriends or practised more self-control.

- Like opening a present before Christmas, sex before marriage spoils things when the right time comes. If you avoid it, you will also save yourself from making comparisons when you are married. If you keep sexual intimacy for the person you marry, you will save yourself a lot of guilt, pain and regret.

Aim for the best

You will not be alone in wanting to follow a life that honours God. You are likely to find help from other Christians among your family, church or friends. Once you have left home, it might be good to look for a godly friend, usually of the same sex with whom you can share your thoughts in this area of your life.[14]

We now live in a culture where sexual intimacy is considered more as a right or a recreation than God's gift for the special relationship of marriage. Your friends may say that you are missing out by keeping sex for marriage, but do not be deceived. Keep yourself, your desires and your body for your future wife or husband if you later get married, and in holiness for God if you don't. The Bible promises fruitfulness, blessing and strength for those who follow God's ways (Psalms 127 and 128). 'Blessed is everyone who fears the Lord, who walks in his ways!' (Psalm 128:1).

9

Marriage

We have looked at six issues that have a common thread. At their heart they distort or disregard God's design for men and women, for marriage and for sexual purity. In all this confusion, there are two questions that might have arisen in your mind – why is marriage so important, and how and why is it under attack?

Why is marriage so important?

It is a striking fact that marriage has been recorded throughout history and in nations, religions and cultures all around the world, where it is usually the fundamental unit of society, as it has been in our own nation.

Marriage is important because it was designed by God. We have already mentioned how, in the book of Genesis, God brought Eve to Adam as his wife, to be his companion and helper. Adam and Eve were told by God to have children, and in this way to fill the earth and to subdue it. In Genesis

2:24 (NIVUK), God gives the pattern for marriage: 'a man leaves his father and mother and is united to his wife, and they become one flesh'. Marriage involves leaving parents and uniting as husband and wife. This 'uniting' works out in a number of ways – practically (for example, living under one roof), emotionally (caring for each other and sharing the ups and downs of life together) and physically (that is, sexually). God designed sexual intimacy to bless marriage by strengthening the emotional bond of love and by making it fruitful in conceiving children. His direction to keep sexual intimacy for marriage ensures that children are born and brought up by their parents in a secure and loving home.

God designed men and women to be attracted to one another and sometimes these feelings may lead to marriage. But love in marriage is not just a strong feeling. The Bible describes the relationship of marriage as a covenant (Malachi 2:14).[1] It is a permanent commitment between the two people getting married based on their promises to love and be faithful to each other until one of them dies. This covenant of marriage gives security. In marriage, over time, the high intensity of the initial attraction and romance will develop into a deep trust and continuing commitment.

We see the goodness of God's design in the benefits marriage brings to society, as well as to the couple themselves. Marriage has been called the building block of society. Strong buildings are made of well-chosen bricks or stones. In the same way, communities are built on the blocks of family units based on marriage. Without strong marriages and families, the foundations of society become unstable, and communities start to fall apart.

There are many practical benefits to being married. It provides help and companionship in sharing the duties and difficulties of life. Married couples are, on average, healthier and more economically prosperous than those in other types of relationships.

Marriage is not only important because of all its practical benefits. We can see how important marriage is to God because the Bible uses it as a picture of the most precious relationship of Jesus Christ and his church (Ephesians 5:31–32).[2] This is perhaps why marriage is sometimes called *holy* matrimony. It is interesting that the Bible starts with a wedding (Genesis 2:24), Jesus' first miracle was at a wedding (John 2:1–11) and the Bible ends with what is called the wedding supper of the Lamb, when Jesus Christ is fully united with his church at the end of the world (Revelation 19:9).[3] Marriage could be described as a 'trailer' for heaven. God's creation of marriage is inextricably linked to the gospel which brings Christ into a relationship with his church – anything that attacks marriage is also attacking the gospel.

From this short summary of the importance of marriage, we can see why Satan has reason to hate, and so to attack, marriage – in doing so he seeks to undermine its good design, damage loving companionship, family life, strong societies and, most of all, discredit the gospel. How is Satan putting his hatred of marriage into action?

Marriage is under attack

Within society

There have been attacks on marriage at various times in history. In more recent times and particularly since the 18th century, at a time called the Enlightenment, some people began to promote and practise their own ideas about marriage rather than accepting what is taught in the Bible. As time went on, even students of the Bible started judging what God said about marriage and sexuality on the basis of their own reasoning or feelings. Because of this and other influences, with the coming of the sexual revolution in the 1960s, sexuality and sexual activity have increasingly been separated from the joining of a man and woman in marriage and from the procreation of children.

At school, PSHE and Sex Education lessons are likely to give only a brief mention of marriage and deny the importance of keeping sex for marriage. Marriage is seldom mentioned in the media and, if it is, it is often with a negative bias.

The current sexual culture promotes intimacy before marriage. There has been a huge rise in the number of couples in a cohabiting relationship (see chapter 2, *Cohabitation*). There has been an increased use of the internet, images and ideas that provoke sexual arousal outside marriage and which raise false expectations about intimacy (see chapter 3, *Pornography*).

The advent of contraception has made it easier to be sexually active outside marriage without risking pregnancy.

Abortion (see chapter 7) has been made available to 'deal' with the unwanted pregnancies that still occur. Easy divorce laws have made people less motivated to work hard when difficulties arise in marriages.

Further serious attacks have struck at the very nature of marriage itself. God designed marriage to be between a man and a woman, who are both physically and emotionally different. In marriage these differences are designed to be complementary and strengthen the marriage.

Homosexuality (see chapter 4) rejects this design by practising sexual intimacy between those of the same sex. Modern feminism (see chapter 6, *Men and women*) rejects this design in another way by trying to make the role of women and men the same, rather than complementary. More recently, the essential distinctions between being a man and a woman are being blurred by the transgender movement (see chapter 5, *Gender identity*).

Individually

Such a sexual culture has hurt many young people who later regret previous sexual experiences. Many are left wondering whether they will be worthy of respect in a future relationship and whether another relationship could be different or could last.

Many young people are experiencing pain from parental divorce and family breakdown. This makes them wonder if there is any point in getting married at all. It also means that fewer young people have a good example of marriage to follow. The upsurge of individualism in society has made it more difficult for people to love each other in a self-sacrificial way. Building a marriage takes effort, requiring a husband and wife to be unselfish and prioritise their marriage over their own agendas.

But don't be put off: marriage is good. It is designed by a wise and loving God. Most people are right to long for what marriage offers – unconditional love and companionship through the different stages of life. In the next chapter we will look at what can help you make a good marriage which survives the stresses and strains of daily life.

10

The gifts of singleness and marriage

Singleness – a special gift

At your age and stage of life, it is likely that you are single (by this we mean not married, rather than not in a relationship). In fact, in both the UK and the US, without your parents' consent you cannot marry in law until you are 18 years old. Even when you reach 18, there are reasons why it may not be wise to marry too quickly. For example, you may not have met a person who you will be happy to spend the rest of your life with, or you may not be ready to handle the responsibilities that come with marriage and the possibility of bringing up children.

The Bible outlines two, and only two, states of living as an adult – either single (and sexually inactive), or married (and sexually active). Everyone starts single, but you may at some stage, by God's choosing, move to the other state! And, of course, people move from being married to being single again if their husband or wife dies.

Singleness and marriage are both gifts from God who is sovereign over all our circumstances. Being single allows a person to serve God without some of the responsibilities that come with marriage and family life (1 Corinthians 7:32–34), sometimes in a way that is impossible for the married person.[1] Dr Helen Roseveare, who studied medicine in the 1940s, had a long career as a missionary doctor in the Congo. As a single woman she was able to demonstrate God's love and care to many throughout her life, both in her medical work and, afterwards, in her books and travels talking about her experiences.

God designed us to live in community, and so some single people may feel lonely. However, most single people find that they can develop a range of friendships in which they can both give and receive support. It is encouraging to know that God orders our lives and determines how and where we will serve him. He can give us the strength to serve him and to be content in whatever circumstances we find ourselves. The Apostle Paul, as a single person, found contentment in his circumstances (which included imprisonment)! He says, 'I can do all things through him [Christ] who strengthens me' (Philippians 4:13). Jesus Christ lived the most perfectly fulfilled life as a single person during his earthly ministry. He is our best example and greatest friend.

Marriage – another special gift

Most young people, especially Christians, would like to get married sometime in the future. It is certainly good to be open to getting married and to explore this possibility at the right stage of life. Proverbs 18:22 holds out the reward: 'He who finds a wife finds a good thing and obtains favour from the Lord.' When young people are considering marriage, they often wonder if they could really commit to loving the same person for the rest of their lives or whether their desires or needs will change with time. They might doubt their ability to keep to the promises made in the marriage vows. If you have these concerns, it is helpful to remember that marriage is God's design, which he describes as 'good'. God himself is committed to building up and sustaining the couple whom he has joined together (Matthew 19:6).[2] If you follow his wisdom and commandments, you will enjoy his blessings in marriage. If you are engaged and planning to get married, it is also a good idea to take part in a marriage preparation course or to have some discussions with an older happily married couple you feel comfortable with.

Here is some practical advice to help you have a happy marriage and respect the marriages of others. You may think marriage is a long way off, but these points are worth taking to heart as you look ahead to the possibility of marriage in the future, and as you relate to married couples in your family or your church.

Understand marriage is precious

The Bible makes it clear that marriage is to be guarded and treasured (Hebrews 13:4).[3] Some people have compared marriage to a very precious vase which should be protected from damage. This perspective will transform the way that the married couple act towards each other in order to avoid any division or threat from outside.

Because marriage is precious, we should also respect and support other people's marriages. Although few people think about it, one of the reasons that family and friends are invited to witness a couple's wedding is so that they can support the couple if difficulties arise for them in the years to come. We should be careful never to say or do anything that might undermine someone else's marriage. Sometimes there are things we could do to help a married couple who are going through a difficult or especially busy time. As well as praying for them, people in churches may, for example, arrange to drop off meals for a family where a new baby has been born or when someone in the home is seriously ill.

Leaving parents

The Bible teaches us that when we marry, we need to leave our parents. This is why the father 'gives away' his daughter in the marriage ceremony. All sorts of difficulties can arise in a marriage if the couple fail to leave home, either emotionally or practically, to form a new family. However, it is often the parents who do not let their children go. This can be hard as a parent, but necessary in order to let the new marriage flourish. This does not mean parents should not be prepared to support or help their children, especially if they become grandparents, but they should not attempt to have authority in the new home.

Unity in marriage

The Bible teaches that the married couple are to unite their lives and their bodies in what is described as a 'one flesh' relationship (Genesis 2:24). Marriage should not consist of two people living in parallel, as our individualistic society might desire, but of two people living as one in all areas of life. Each works towards the good of both – we have described the different roles and responsibilities for the husband and wife in chapter 6. The outworking of this uniting of lives is often very practical: sharing a house, a surname, bank accounts, holidays, cars, meals, etc. But unity must be deeper too: sharing values (and you need to talk about these long before you get married), emotions, and a deep level of trust.

For the Christian, this unity involves sharing in and living out your personal faith in Jesus Christ, which radically impacts all areas of life. The Bible warns about the impossibility of true unity between a believer and a non-believer (2 Corinthians 6:14).[4] Marriages that attempt this are usually painful and compromised. Because of this a Christian should not go out with a non-believer, since the purpose of going out is to see if marriage is an option. In the Old Testament, the intermarriage of God's people with those who did not worship the only true God led them to worship idols. Consider what happened to Solomon and Samson (1 Kings 11:1–6 and Judges 16:4–20).

Commitment

Commitment brings both security and satisfaction to a marriage. Such commitment involves self-sacrifice, not self-fulfilment (love 'does not insist on its own way', 1 Corinthians 13:5). There will be times when it is necessary for the couple to express love by patiently working at the relationship ('Love bears all things, believes all things,' 1 Corinthians 13:7) and so keep the promises that they made to each other at the wedding, even if they do not feel like it. The words in the marriage vows, 'for better, for worse', sum up love in marriage which is unconditional.

Married couples should always look to forgive and not hold onto grievances. The Bible warns us: 'do not let the sun go down on your anger, and give no opportunity to the devil' (Ephesians 4:26–27). A couple should never go to sleep with a grudge against their spouse.

Kind words, not point-scoring

It is very easy to want to score points or to try to put each other down in some subtle way. It is important to avoid this, but rather to see the best in the other and make the most gracious interpretation of their words and actions. Married couples should remember to speak kind words of appreciation and show gratitude to each other – both when they are with other people and when they are on their own. In this way it is possible to give each other an atmosphere in which to grow.

Loyalty

A married couple are to be loyal to each other, and not be tempted to say or do anything behind each other's backs. There should be nothing on a phone, computer or in social media that a married couple would not be happy for each other to see.

Sexual intimacy

Sexual intimacy is an important part of marriage. It is a physical, emotional and spiritual expression of the 'one flesh' unity of marriage (Genesis 2:24).

One essential expression of loyalty is the need to be sexually faithful in marriage. In a traditional wedding service, the couple getting married promise to 'forsake all others', meaning they promise to give up the opportunity of having a sexual relationship with another person. If a married person has sex with someone who is not their wife or husband, this is called adultery. The seventh commandment warns us 'You shall not commit adultery' (Exodus 20:14). The Bible often compares adultery to the unfaithfulness of God's people in worshipping idols. Adultery damages and may even destroy marriage.

The Bible tells us to avoid sexual immorality

(1 Corinthians 6:18), which includes sexual arousal before marriage.[5] This is one reason why cohabitation is wrong. As a couple get to know each other before marriage, they should do everything possible to show self-control and build up trust. Sadly, some Christian couples become intimately involved and allow themselves to become sexually aroused before marriage and then need to draw back. This is not only wrong but can set up a pattern of response that then spills over into marriage. Instead of being able to relax and enjoy sexual intimacy within marriage, the brakes go on when the time is right, and this makes sexual intimacy within marriage more difficult. The foundation for a healthy and godly marriage starts to be built during the time the couple are going out.

Avoid making each other an idol

A married couple need to be careful not to expect their spouse to meet all their emotional and spiritual needs; that is too much to expect from one person. Only God can meet those deeper needs. If a person's basic need for security, significance and self-worth is met by God, then they will be free to live for God and for their spouse, not only for themselves.

Thoughtfulness

Each partner in the marriage should consider the needs of the other. It can be difficult to live in a way that prioritises the marriage over our own plans and ideas. We all tend to assume that our way of thinking or doing is best, but in marriage there needs to be adjustment. This is particularly true if someone gets married after leaving home and enjoying an independent life as a student or an employee. It can also be difficult if someone has never seen unity in marriage in their own family as they have grown up.

Thoughtfulness has its outworking in the practicalities of everyday life. Think how someone's actions and reactions impact the other person. Even small things can be really annoying! For example, dropping clothes on the floor and expecting someone else to pick them up or not putting the top on the toothpaste! When we're thoughtful in the small things, little by little it becomes part of our character.

Talking to each other

If you are wondering whether someone will make a suitable marriage partner, consider whether you can open your heart and mind to them as you would do with a close friend. In spite of the busyness of life, it is important to take time in marriage to talk together. As with any friendship, a couple need to remember to make eye contact when they are discussing something (driving excepted!) and avoid distractions from their phone or the TV.

Helping each other

One of the Bible's descriptions of a wife is as a 'helper' (Genesis 2:18). The Bible also describes God as our helper (Psalm 54:4; Hebrews 13:6).[6] Helping each other in marriage is very important. People often end up marrying someone who is complementary to them in personality and skills, as well as, of course, being the opposite sex. The husband and wife can help each other both in practical tasks and by giving each other emotional support.

Difficulties may test the marriage and will reveal weaknesses and strengths in each other, but overcoming difficulties together helps build a deeper and more solid relationship. Commitment allows a couple to stand together and face the world.

Final comments – looking ahead

We have repeated several times in the pages of this book that God designed marriage as the basis for family life. He planned that one man and one woman would promise to stay together as husband and wife and love each other for the rest of their lives. This is how families began and still begin today. This book has covered topics that challenge God's original design for marriage and the family from several angles. Our prayer is that this book will encourage you to face such challenges with a confidence that God's ways are always best.

Endnotes

Chapter 2: Cohabitation

1. The statistics quoted relate to opposite sex cohabiting couple families. 'Families and households in the UK: 2021', Table 1, ONS, 9 March 2022, see https://www.ons.gov.uk/peoplepopulationandcommunity/birthsdeathsandmarriages/families/bulletins/familiesandhouseholds/2021

2. *Historical Living Arrangements of Adults*, Table UC-1: Unmarried Couples of the Opposite-Sex: 1960 to Present, United Census Bureau, November 2021, see https://www.census.gov/data/tables/time-series/demo/families/adults.html

3. 'Marriage statistics, cohabitation and cohort analyses', Table 1, ONS, 11 June 2014, see https://www.ons.gov.uk/peoplepopulationandcommunity/birthsdeathsandmarriages/marriagecohabitationandcivilpartnerships/datasets/marriagestatisticscohabitationandcohortanalyses

4. P Hemez and W D Manning, 'Thirty years of change in women's premarital cohabitation experience', *Family Profile* No. 5, 2017, Bowling Green, OH: National Center for Family & Marriage Research.

5. *Vows and promises for your wedding*, Oxfordshire County Council, see https://tinyurl.com/Oxfordmarriagevows and *Standard Courthouse Wedding Vows for Your City Hall Ceremony*, Choco Studio Photography,

see https://www.chocostudio.com/city-hall/standard-courthouse-wedding-vows/

6. The Church of England, *Common Worship: Pastoral Services* (Church House Publishing, 2000, 2005). See also https://www.churchofengland.org/prayer-and-worship/worship-texts-and-resources/common-worship/marriage

7. *No fault divorce – UK divorce changes explained*, Co-op Legal Services, see https://www.co-oplegalservices.co.uk/family-law-solicitors/divorce/no-fault-divorce-uk-law-change/

8. 'Who shall dwell on your holy hill? He… in whose eyes a vile person is despised, but who honours those who fear the Lord; who swears to his own hurt and does not change' (Psalm 15:1b–2, 4).

9. Image created by Rtyu1120 and Ssolbergj and used from Wikimedia Commons under the terms of the Creative Commons Attribution-ShareAlike 4.0 licence.

10. Dietrich Bonhoeffer, 'Wedding Sermon from the Prison Cell', *Letters and Papers from Prison* (Fortress Press, 2010), p. 84.

11. *Marriage and Civil Partnership in England and Wales*, Government Equalities Office, 10 December 2019, see https://assets.publishing.service.gov.uk/government/uploads/system/uploads/attachment_data/file/851152/Marriage_and_Civil_Partnership_in_England_and_Wales.pdf and Las Vegas Defense Group Family Law Division, *5 differences between marriage and domestic partnership in Nevada*, Shouse California Law Group, see https://www.shouselaw.com/nv/family/marriage-vs-domestic-partnership/

12. *'Common law marriage' and cohabitation*, House of Commons Library, Briefing Paper 03372, 4 May 2021.

13. 'He answered, "Have you not read that he who created them from the beginning made them male and female, and said, 'Therefore a man shall leave his father and his mother and hold fast to his wife, and the two shall become one flesh'?"' (Matthew 19:4–5).

14. 'Flee from sexual immorality. Every other sin a person commits is outside the body, but the sexually immoral person sins against his own body. Or do you not know that your body is a temple of the

Holy Spirit within you, whom you have from God? You are not your own, for you were bought with a price. So glorify God in your body' (1 Corinthians 6:18–20). 'But if they cannot exercise self-control, they should marry. For it is better to marry than to burn with passion' (1 Corinthians 7:9).

15. Michael Rosenfeld and Katharina Roesler, 'Cohabitation Experience and Cohabitation's Association with Marital Dissolution', *Journal of Marriage and Family*, Vol 81, Issue 1, pp. 42–58.

16. *Marriage and cohabitation (General Lifestyle Survey Overview - a report on the 2011 General Lifestyle Survey)*, Office for National Statistics, 7 March 2013, section 5, see https://tinyurl.com/ONScohabitationduration

17. Alicia VanOrman, *Cohabiting Couples in the United States Are Staying Together Longer but Fewer Are Marrying*, Population Reference Bureau, 5 November 2020, see https://www.prb.org/resources/cohabiting-couple-staying-together-longer/

18. 'What Percentage of Marriages End in Divorce?', ONS, The National Archives, 9 February 2013, see https://webarchive.nationalarchives.gov.uk/ukgwa/20160106011951/http://www.ons.gov.uk/ons/rel/vsob1/divorces-in-england-and-wales/2011/sty-what-percentage-of-marriages-end-in-divorce.html and 'Divorce Statistics: Over 115 Studies, Facts and Rates for 2022', Wilkinson and Finkbeiner, https://tinyurl.com/marriagesendingdivorce

19. 'Forgotten Families? The Vanishing Agenda', Centre for Social Justice, October 2012, p. 8.

20. Richard Reeves, *Parenting, Cam Newton and Marriage vs Cohabitation*, Brookings, 12 January 2016, see https://www.brookings.edu/opinions/parenting-cam-newton-and-marriage-vs-cohabitation/

21. Harry Benson, *Establishing the facts about family breakdown, transforming the debate about marriage*, Marriage Foundation, July 2017, p. 1.

22. R Reeves and E Krause, *Cohabiting Parents Differ from Married Ones in Three Big Ways*, Brookings, 5 April 2017, see https://www.brookings.edu/research/cohabiting-parents-differ-from-married-ones-in-three-big-ways/

23. 'Families and Households in the UK: 2021', ONS, 9 March 2022, see https://www.ons.gov.uk/peoplepopulationandcommunity/birthsdeathsandmarriages/families/bulletins/familiesandhouseholds/2021

24. *The Majority of Children Live with Two Parents, Census Bureau Reports*, United States Census Bureau, 17 November 2016, see https://www.census.gov/newsroom/press-releases/2016/cb16-192.html and Stephanie Kramer, *U.S. Has World's Highest Rate of Children Living in Single-Parent Households*, Pew Research Center, 12 December 2019, see https://www.pewresearch.org/fact-tank/2019/12/12/u-s-children-more-likely-than-children-in-other-countries-to-live-with-just-one-parent/

25. D Busby, J Carroll and B Willoughby, 'Compatibility or restraint? The effects of sexual timing on marriage relationships', *Journal of Family Psychology*, Vol 24, No 6, December 2010, pp. 766–774.

26. Prof J Boivin, *A Guide to Fertility: At what age does fertility begin to decrease?* British Fertility Society, see https://www.britishfertilitysociety.org.uk/fei/at-what-age-does-fertility-begin-to-decrease/

Chapter 3: Pornography

1. Lovewise Online, *What is wrong with masturbation?*, 16 August 2019, see lovewiseonline.org/what-is-wrong-with-masturbation/

2. '…on those parts of the body that we think less honourable we bestow the greater honour, and our unpresentable parts are treated with greater modesty' (1 Corinthians 12:23).

3. *Sharing nudes and semi-nudes: advice for education settings working with children and young people*, Gov.uk, 23 December 2020, 1.7–1.9, see https://www.gov.uk/government/publications/sharing-nudes-and-semi-nudes-advice-for-education-settings-working-with-children-and-young-people

4. 'And [Jesus] said to him, "You shall love the Lord your God with all your heart and with all your soul and with all your mind"' (Matthew 22:37).

5. 'You shall not commit adultery' (Exodus 20:14). 'For the wife does not have authority over her own body, but the husband does. Likewise the husband does not have authority over his own body, but the wife does' (1 Corinthians 7:4).

6. 'I made a covenant with my eyes not to look lustfully at a young woman' (Job 31:1, NIVUK).

7. 'If your right eye causes you to sin, tear it out and throw it away. For it is better that you lose one of your members than that your whole body be thrown into hell. And if your right hand causes you to sin, cut it off and throw it away. For it is better that you lose one of your members than that your whole body go into hell' (Matthew 5:29–30).

Chapter 4: Homosexuality

1. In 2019, 93.7% of the adult population identified as heterosexual or straight. 'Sexual orientation, UK: 2019', ONS, 27 May 2021, see https://tinyurl.com/sexualidentity2019

2. 'He answered, "Have you not read that he who created them from the beginning made them male and female, and said, 'Therefore a man shall leave his father and his mother and hold fast to his wife, and the two shall become one flesh'?"' (Matthew 19:4–5).

3. 'We destroy arguments and every lofty opinion raised against the knowledge of God, and take every thought captive to obey Christ' (2 Corinthians 10:5).

4. 'I press on towards the goal for the prize of the upward call of God in Christ Jesus' (Philippians 3:14).

Chapter 5: Gender identity

1. See for example, Judith Butler, *Gender Trouble: Feminism and the Subversion of Identity* (Routledge, 2006).

2. Gender dysphoria is not to be confused with so-called 'intersex' conditions, which are present at birth, and caused by chromosomal, hormonal or developmental abnormalities leading to an ambiguity of biological sex. In managing these, both parents and doctors seek to

identify the true – or, when uncertain, most likely – sex and provide medical interventions to help the child to develop and function as normally as possible in that sex.

3. Simon Baron-Cohen, *The Essential Difference: Men, Women and the Extreme Male Brain* (Penguin, 2012).

4. 'Besides that, they learn to be idlers, going about from house to house, and not only idlers, but also gossips and busybodies, saying what they should not' (1 Timothy 5:13).

5. 'I desire then that in every place the men should pray, lifting holy hands without anger or quarrelling' (1 Timothy 2:8).

6. Riittakerttu Kaltiala-Heino et al, 'Gender dysphoria in adolescence: current perspectives (Childhood GD and puberty development)', *Adolescent Health, Medicine and Therapeutics*, 9, 2018, pp. 31–41. Also Paul Hruz, Lawrence Mayer and Paul McHugh, 'Growing Pains - Problems with Puberty Suppression in Treating Gender Dysphoria', *The New Atlantis*, 52, Spring 2017, p. 19.

7. C Richards, J Maxwell and N McCune, 'Use of puberty blockers for gender dysphoria: a momentous step in the dark', Letter, *Archives of Disease in Childhood*, 17 January 2019.

8. Polly Carmichael et al, 'Short-term outcomes of pubertal suppression in a selected cohort of 12-to-15-year old young people with persistent gender dysphoria in the UK', *PLOS ONE*, 2 February 2021.

9. Philip Cheng et al, 'Fertility concerns of the transgender patient', *Translational Andrology and Urology*, June 2019, Vol 8, No 3, pp. 209–218.

10. Abigail Shrier, *Irreversible Damage: The Transgender Craze Seducing Our Daughters* (Washington: Regnery Publishing, 2020), p. 170.

11. 'You shall not commit adultery' (Exodus 20:14).

12. 'A woman must not wear men's clothing, nor a man wear women's clothing, for the Lord your God detests anyone who does this' (Deuteronomy 22:5, NIVUK).

13. 'I myself in my mind am a slave to God's law, but in my sinful nature a slave to the law of sin' (Romans 7:25, NIVUK).

14. Lovewise Online, 'Social media and gender identity', 23 November 2020, see https://lovewiseonline.org/social-media-and-gender-identity/

15. 'He heals the broken-hearted and binds up their wounds' (Psalm 147:3).

16. 'Come to me, all who labour and are heavy laden, and I will give you rest' (Matthew 11:28). 'Therefore, if anyone is in Christ, he is a new creation. The old has passed away; behold, the new has come' (2 Corinthians 5:17).

17. 'He said, "I have been very jealous for the Lord, the God of hosts. For the people of Israel have forsaken your covenant, thrown down your altars, and killed your prophets with the sword, and I, even I only, am left, and they seek my life, to take it away." [And the Lord said to him,] "Yet I will leave seven thousand in Israel, all the knees that have not bowed to Baal, and every mouth that has not kissed him"' (1 Kings 19:14, 18).

18. 'For I know the plans I have for you, declares the Lord, plans for welfare and not for evil, to give you a future and a hope' (Jeremiah 29:11).

Chapter 6: Men and women

1. 'Then the man said, "This at last is bone of my bones and flesh of my flesh; she shall be called Woman, because she was taken out of Man"' (Genesis 2:23).

2. 'But the Lord God called to the man and said to him, "Where are you?" And he said, "I heard the sound of you in the garden, and I was afraid, because I was naked, and I hid myself." He said, "Who told you that you were naked? Have you eaten of the tree of which I commanded you not to eat?"' (Genesis 3:9–11).

3. For a further discussion of feminism, see Part II of *God's Design for Women in an Age of Gender Confusion* by Sharon James, Evangelical Press, 2019.

4. 'Blessed be the God and Father of our Lord Jesus Christ, who has blessed us in Christ with every spiritual blessing in the heavenly places, even as he chose us in him before the foundation of the

world, that we should be holy and blameless before him. In love he predestined us for adoption as sons through Jesus Christ, according to the purpose of his will, to the praise of his glorious grace, with which he has blessed us in the Beloved' (Ephesians 1:3–6).

5. 'But I want you to understand that the head of every man is Christ, the head of a wife is her husband, and the head of Christ is God' (1 Corinthians 11:3).

6. 'He does not deal with us according to our sins, nor repay us according to our iniquities' (Psalm 103:10).

7. Karen Swallow Prior, *Fierce Convictions: The Extraordinary life of Hannah More – Poet, Reformer, Abolitionist* (Nashville: Nelson Books, 2014); Sarah Allen, *Hannah More: the woman who wouldn't stop writing* (Inverness: Christian Focus Publications, 2014); and Sharon James, *Ann Judson: A Missionary Life for Burma* (Welwyn Garden City: EP Books, 2016).

8. 'I wish that all were as I myself am. But each has his own gift from God, one of one kind and one of another' (1 Corinthians 7:7).

9. For excellent and readable summaries of such men, see Iain H Murray (ed.), *Five Pioneer Missionaries*, (Banner of Truth, 1965); Brian H Cosby, *David Brainerd: a love for the lost* (Inverness: Christian Focus Publications, 2011).

10. For an encouraging account of these, see Peter Lupson, *In God's Company: Christian Giants of Business* (Leominster: DayOne, 2019).

11. '...and so train the young women to love their husbands and children, to be self-controlled, pure, working at home, kind, and submissive to their own husbands, that the word of God may not be reviled' (Titus 2:4–5). 'Yet she will be saved through childbearing – if they continue in faith and love and holiness, with self-control' (1 Timothy 2:15).

12. '...women should adorn themselves in respectable apparel, with modesty and self-control, not with braided hair and gold or pearls or costly attire, but with what is proper for women who profess godliness – with good works' (1 Timothy 2:9–10).

13. 'A new commandment I give to you, that you love one another: just as I have loved you, you also are to love one another' (John 13:34).

'Love one another with brotherly affection. Outdo one another in showing honour' (Romans 12:10).

Chapter 7: Abortion

1. 'For behold, when the sound of your greeting came to my ears, the baby in my womb leaped for joy' (Luke 1:44).

2. Sometimes this verse is wrongly understood as referring to his mother's sin of conception. The psalm's context shows that David was referring to his own sin.

3. 'Give justice to the weak and the fatherless; maintain the right of the afflicted and the destitute' (Psalm 82:3).

4. Alvin Schmidt, *How Christianity Changed the World* (Grand Rapids: Zondervan, 2004), pp. 57–60; for a shorter summary of a similar account read Sharon James, *How Christianity Transformed the World* (Inverness: Christian Focus Publications, 2021), p. 73.

5. Department of Health and Social Care, *National Statistics: Abortion Statistics for England and Wales: 2020*, 31 August 2021.

6. Katherine Kortsmit et al, *Abortion Surveillance – United States, 2019*, CDC Morbidity and Mortality Weekly Report, 26 November 2021, Vol 70, No. 9, pp. 1–29, see https://www.cdc.gov/mmwr/volumes/70/ss/ss7009a1.htm

7. Department of Health and Social Care, *Abortion statistics 2020: data tables*, Table 1 and *Terminations of pregnancy by age group: 1968–2020*, Termination of Pregnancy Statistics, year ending December 2020, Public Health Scotland, May 2021, Table 7.

8. *Number of legal abortions reported in the US from 1973 to 2019*, Statista.com, see https://www.statista.com/statistics/185274/number-of-legal-abortions-in-the-us-since-2000/

9. 'Conceptions in England and Wales: 2020', ONS, 14 April 2022 and Rachel K Jones, Elizabeth Witwer and Jenna Jerman, *Abortion Incidence and Service Availability in the United States, 2017*, Guttmacher Institute, September 2019, see https://www.guttmacher.org/report/abortion-incidence-service-availability-us-2017

10. Human Fertilisation and Embryology Act 1990, Section 37(1)(d),

see https://www.legislation.gov.uk/ukpga/1990/37/section/37/enacted

11. 'Gestation' is defined as the time in the womb since fertilisation. This is two weeks shorter than the duration termed 'so many weeks pregnant' which is calculated from the first day of the woman's last menstrual period.

12. Stuart W G Derbyshire and John C Bockmann, 'Reconsidering Fetal Pain', *Journal of Medical Ethics* Vol 46, No 1, 14 January 2020, see https://jme.bmj.com/content/46/1/3 and Martin Ward Platt, 'Fetal awareness and fetal pain: the Emperor's new clothes', *Archive of Disease in Childhood: Fetal & Neonatal* Vol 96, No 4, 12 June 2011, see https://fn.bmj.com/content/96/4/F236

13. 'In love he predestined us for adoption as sons through Jesus Christ, according to the purpose of his will' (Ephesians 1:4–5).

14. For example, Psalm 82:3–4 reads: 'Give justice to the weak and the fatherless; maintain the right of the afflicted and the destitute. Rescue the weak and the needy; deliver them from the hand of the wicked.'

15. For example, Ben and Valentina Cadoux-Hudson and Dr Chris Richards, *Thinking about Abortion: Where do we begin?* (Leyland: Evangelical Press, 2021), pp. 42, 91, 103, 107.

16. 'He does not deal with us according to our sins, nor repay us according to our iniquities. For as high as the heavens are above the earth, so great is his steadfast love toward those who fear him; as far as the east is from the west, so far does he remove our transgressions from us' (Psalm 103:10–12).

17. Cadoux-Hudson and Richards, *Thinking about Abortion: Where do we begin?* pp. 104–109.

18. Mary Lou, taken from a testimony from the DVD 'Silent No More', produced by British Victims of Abortion, April 2006, with permission.

Chapter 8: Personal purity

1. 'Be not wise in your own eyes; fear the Lord, and turn away from evil' (Proverbs 3:7).

2. 'If we confess our sins, he is faithful and just to forgive us our sins and to cleanse us from all unrighteousness' (1 John 1:9).

3. 'There is therefore now no condemnation for those who are in Christ Jesus' (Romans 8:1).

4. 'Jesus answered him, "If anyone loves me, he will keep my word, and my Father will love him, and we will come to him and make our home with him"' (John 14:23).

5. 'But the fruit of the Spirit is love, joy, peace, patience, kindness, goodness, faithfulness, gentleness, self-control; against such things there is no law' (Galatians 5:22–23).

6. '...praying at all times in the Spirit, with all prayer and supplication. To that end, keep alert with all perseverance, making supplication for all the saints' (Ephesians 6:18).

7. 'You have heard that it was said, "You shall not commit adultery." But I say to you that everyone who looks at a woman with lustful intent has already committed adultery with her in his heart' (Matthew 5:27–28).

8. 'If you obey the commandments of the Lord your God that I command you today, by loving the Lord your God, by walking in his ways, and by keeping his commandments and his statutes and his rules, then you shall live and multiply, and the Lord your God will bless you in the land that you are entering to take possession of it' (Deuteronomy 30:16). 'If your law had not been my delight, I would have perished in my affliction' (Psalm 119:92).

9. 'So flee youthful passions and pursue righteousness, faith, love, and peace, along with those who call on the Lord from a pure heart' (2 Timothy 2:22). 'Flee from sexual immorality. Every other sin a person commits is outside the body, but the sexually immoral person sins against his own body' (1 Corinthians 6:18).

10. '...she caught him by his garment, saying, "Lie with me." But he left his garment in her hand and fled and got out of the house' (Genesis 39:12).

11. 'But he does not know that the dead are there, that her guests are in the depths of Sheol' (Proverbs 9:18).

12. 'And God saw everything that he had made, and behold, it was very good' (Genesis 1:31).

13. *True Love Interactive Bible Study*, Lovewise, see https://lovewise.org.uk/true-love-videos/marrying-right-reasons

14. Sometimes called an accountability partner.

Chapter 9: Marriage

1. 'But you say, "Why does he not?" Because the Lord was witness between you and the wife of your youth, to whom you have been faithless, though she is your companion and your wife by covenant' (Malachi 2:14).

2. '"Therefore a man shall leave his father and mother and hold fast to his wife, and the two shall become one flesh." This mystery is profound, and I am saying that it refers to Christ and the church' (Ephesians 5:31–32).

3. 'And the angel said to me, "Write this: Blessed are those who are invited to the marriage supper of the Lamb." And he said to me, "These are the true words of God."'(Revelation 19:9).

Chapter 10: The gifts of singleness and marriage

1. 'I want you to be free from anxieties. The unmarried man is anxious about the things of the Lord, how to please the Lord. But the married man is anxious about worldly things, how to please his wife, and his interests are divided. And the unmarried or betrothed woman is anxious about the things of the Lord, how to be holy in body and spirit. But the married woman is anxious about worldly things, how to please her husband' (1 Corinthians 7:32–34).

2. 'So they are no longer two but one flesh. What therefore God has joined together, let not man separate' (Matthew 19:6).

3. 'Let marriage be held in honour among all, and let the marriage bed be undefiled, for God will judge the sexually immoral and adulterous' (Hebrews 13:4).

4. 'Do not be unequally yoked with unbelievers. For what partnership has righteousness with lawlessness? Or what fellowship has light with darkness?' (2 Corinthians 6:14).

5. 'Flee from sexual immorality. Every other sin a person commits

is outside the body, but the sexually immoral person sins against his own body' (1 Corinthians 6:18).

6. 'Behold, God is my helper; the Lord is the upholder of my life' (Psalm 54:4). 'So we can confidently say, "The Lord is my helper; I will not fear; what can man do to me?"' (Hebrews 13:6).